PN
2071
·I5
H45

Improvisational Acting

A Handbook of Exercises for the Student Actor

Jack Preston Held

Antelope Valley College

Wadsworth Publishing Company, Inc.
Belmont, California

ST. JOSEPH'S UNIVERSITY

3 9353 00250 9113

This book is gratefully dedicated to

JOSEPH MARSHALL ANDERSON

—an inspiration to all who have

worked with him in the theatre.

©1971 by Wadsworth Publishing Company, Inc.,
Belmont, California 94002. All rights reserved. No
part of this book may be reproduced, stored in a
retrieval system or transcribed, in any form or by
any means, electronic, mechanical, photocopying,
recording, or otherwise, without the prior written
permission of the publisher.

L.C. Cat. Card No.: 79-151074
Printed in the United States of America

1 2 3 4 5 6 7 8 9 10—75 74 73 72 71

Preface

Improvisational Acting is a handbook of exercises leading to self-discovery of the student's potentials in creative acting *and* living; it does not pretend to be a book on acting theories. To make certain that those who are using this book understand its purpose and format, you may wish to read aloud with your group parts or all of the "Introduction."

This book is the first treatment of improvisational acting in ready-reference style, using a semi-outline format for brevity and clarity. Presented in a direct, concise style to reach the widest range of groups, these exercises have been used successfully by beginners and professionals, by adults and young students. Although the exercises are arranged from solo work (Part One) to complex ensembles (Part Two), characterization (Part Three), and finally as rehearsal and performance techniques (Part Four), they can be used experimentally in any order, according to the particular needs of a group. Each category is introduced with a principle and purpose to be achieved and concludes with a set of worksheets for progressive evaluations (often needed but seldom supplied in standard textbooks on acting).

You may want to consult several more comprehensive sources on this subject, prior to using this handbook as a guide to session-planning. Two of the best are John Hodgson and Ernest Richards' *Improvisation: Discovery and Creativity in Drama* and Viola Spolin's *Improvisation for the Theatre: A Handbook of Teaching and Directing Techniques* (see Bibliography at the end of this book). However, you will note that these books are addressed to the teacher-director, rather than the student-actor, which permits them to dwell at some length on the more subtle techniques, psychology, and philosophy of improvisation. They also establish somewhat set patterns of development, which may or may not be of practical service to your particular group.

It is with this personal need and flexibility in mind that this "handbook of exercises" was developed, with your own group needs determining how to arrange the sequence of exercises for effective development. In fact, space is provided for writing in variations of some of the exercises, voluntarily or as assigned.

To apportion your time and energy effectively in using this book, here are some guidelines:

1 Each session should include selections from the four Daily Exercises sets (Part One), starting with the simplest ones and gradually adding more subtle or complex exercises as the group shows progress.

a *Example:*

Warm-Ups 1, 2, 3, 4, 10, 11, 12 (pp. 1-8)

Wake-Ups 1, 2, 7, 8, 9, 15 (pp. 9-14)

Move-Ups 1-*a* thru 1-*h*, 6-*a*, 6-*b* (pp. 17-22)

Speak-Ups 1-*a* (p. 27)

Balance of session in group exercises developing awareness of a specific general weakness in the ensemble (hands? feet? posture? excessive tension?) Use handbook suggestions but always try original variations adapted to your group size and types.

b *Example:* Concentrate whole session on a specific need by selecting those exercises from each set which your group can attempt without undue self-consciousness. Arrange the sequence with simplest private solos first, then partners, then small groups, then large groups, and finally ensemble. Be sure that partnering is varied at each session, so that mutual dependencies do not develop but rather a sense of ensemble begins to unfold.

Always let the needs of your group determine the selection of exercises and types of scenes.

2 Stress awareness at each step. For example, the opportunity to experience two or more senses or emotions simultaneously will occur long before you are ready to concentrate on Change-Ups (Part Two). However, if this is not the specific goal of the present session, do not dwell on the phenomenon, but instead concentrate on awareness of the immediate total experience.

3 On the other hand, try to consider your experiences resulting from solo exercises as personal moments of discovery that should be kept intact and private. If any members of your group volunteer to talk about their discoveries, try to contribute comments which will be helpful to all and which will lead to the next exercise. There will come a time when discussions are desirable, and these are indicated in the text. Even then, criticism will be at a minimum since the purpose of the experience is to enable you to criticize your own approach to a character, to discover the truth about it for yourself, and to learn by doing not by being told right or wrong. Your own instincts and good taste will guide you into recognizing your personal or ensemble weaknesses, as well as your strengths, without any tone of judgment or condemnation arising from evaluations by others.

4 Note the gradualness of the improvisational approach to acting. There will be times when you must meet discouragement with appreciation for thoroughness rather than fall victim to the present-day addiction for "instant" results—all right for making tea or coffee but hardly sufficient for an actor's development. Even if it takes the whole series of sessions for you to comprehend and apply just one principle, such as concentration, it will be time well spent. And the time spent on each exercise, by the way, will be determined by your needs more than by the clock and the calendar.

5 Rehearsal clothing traditionally consists of leotards and sleeveless tops for women, tights and T-shirts for men. Bare feet permit a greater sense of freedom, but athletic socks may be worn if you prefer.

This book could not have been written without the inspiration and guidance of these good people: Esther Mullin, founder of the Curtain Pullers, the Cleveland Playhouse Children's Theatre, where the author first learned about improvisational acting many years ago; Leigh Kentish and Peter Doughty, faculty at the Guildhall School of Music and Drama, London, England, who taught the author how the British theatre utilizes improvisation in training professionals; Students of the 1968-1970 Fundamental and Advanced Acting Classes of Antelope Valley College, Lancaster, California, who encouraged the author to write this book; Paul Miller, who proofread the first draft; Armanda Echenique, who typed the first draft; H. Isis Hilton who typed the final copy; *Photographers*—Dennis Rowlett, Gregory J. Rhoades, Robert McMahan, Advisor; and *Models*—Karen Bradley, Mari Anenberg, David Miniel, James Jones.

Contents

Introduction

This is not really a book "on acting." And how very contradictory it would be even to attempt one on improvisational acting! After all, improvising implies "doing your own thing," not someone else's ideas. However, to save time and effort, here are some exercises in book form to serve as a guide for you and your group. Once you are familiar with the form and style, you can alter the contents to suit your own needs and tastes.

As a participant in an improvisational acting group (be it a class or a club), you will want to be clear on a few principles before you start. First, remember that you are always seeking the truth about what you are doing in these exercises, which are arranged with the simple ones first in each section so that you can experience a gradual awareness of your own potential. You won't have a "performance feeling" in the early exercises because you won't be subjected to criticism or judgment of any kind until later. This will allow you to discover for yourself the truth about yourself and what you are doing. Then as you begin to seek the truth about personalities other than your own, through characterization exercises, you will welcome comments and suggestions from the group to help you convey the truth more clearly to them. In effect, your audience adjustments will begin developing only when you have need for those steps. So do not concern yourself in the early exercises with "performance" or "portrayal" or "communication."

Next, understand that a true experience for the improvisational actor is learned from the outside, and not by looking inwards. It is the awareness of the world around you that causes you to react intellectually and emotionally, just as you hope your audience will react to your interpretation of your experiences.

As you become more totally aware, and capable of interpreting your awareness through ageless artistic disciplines, you will appreciate three faculties long a part of your being, but perhaps somewhat dormant until now: *concentration* (some find this the most challenging faculty to employ fully, because we aren't used to the immersion of our total conscious, attending selves in one encompassing effort); *imagination* (which may have been lost with early childhood, but which we hope to regain in the early exercises); and *observation* (which is, of course, another word for total awareness, with special attention to often overlooked or neglected details of human behavior).

Gradually, as suggested earlier, you will feel the desire to share what your awareness has revealed to you of some truth about human nature. That sense of sharing will be your incentive for further discoveries through the art of acting. At that point, you probably won't have much further need of this book, except as an occasional reminder of this basic principle: be aware, prepare, then share.

There is no monopoly on ideas for improvisational acting, and certainly no one approach to the subject. A national convention of theatre professionals and educators recently met to discuss, among other trends in contemporary theatre, the uses and results of improvisation. But it is hardly a new subject, even though it is just now reaching a universal recognition as a teaching device in many subjects other than acting. British schools, for example, are making use of improvisation in the lower grades, while in California troupes of striking laborers restyle the commedia dell'arte of old Italy as they satirize current social foibles and controversies. However, in this handbook, improvisation is treated mainly as a means to an end (to help the actor convey artistically the communicable truth of his discovery), rather than an end in itself (social commentary or public group therapy).

Remember as you use this handbook that it is a guide, not a rule book. It is brief and direct, avoiding excessive theorizing and explanations in order for you to get immediately to work. Sets of questions are provided to help you evaluate what you've done, and to indicate the type of questions you may wish to discuss with your instructor and fellow-students. Perhaps some extra readings will be necessary to answer these questions, so a list of possible sources is provided in a bibliography at the end. But *acting* is not so much reading as *doing*. It would be best to spend most of your reading time on plays from which you can extract scenes for the exercises in Parts Three and Four. For you who think creatively, a textbook is primarily a means for making your own ideas more tangible. That's what *Improvisational Acting* is for—to encourage you and your group to experiment with creative improvising—a spontaneous means to an artistically disciplined end.

Part One

Daily Exercises

Your body must be a thoroughly disciplined instrument that obeys instantly the command of your will. Through an understanding of tensions and relaxations, you can readily express emotions without inhibiting your body's flexibility. You must maintain a good body tone, be alert to stimuli, and respond with maximum effectiveness but with a minimum of energy. Your body movements must be graceful and facile but thoroughly masculine or feminine in appeal.

All of the following exercises are meant to help you to—

- Relax while engaged in creative action.
- Replace inhibitions with creative awareness.
- Employ your physical senses for creative purposes.
- Stimulate your faculties of concentration, imagination, and observation for creative acting and living.

SECTION ONE

WARM-UPS

To develop awareness of the body as the first medium of communication, you must become aware of how relaxation and tension alternate in movement and gesture. The first ten minutes of every meeting will include a selected routine of the following exercises or variations, all basic for self-discipline in coordinating your mind and body. Only when you have achieved this coordination will you be ready for later exercises in emotional depths.

Always believe what you are doing in these exercises, or else stop until you have cleared your thoughts of doubts and then try again. Forget the "performance complex"—you are not on stage, there is no audience, and you are not auditioning for anything in competition with the other people in your group. Just believe it, enjoy it, and remember it. Don't waste energy in laughter or chatter.

**Building an Action to a
State of Exhaustion**

1 The Handshaker Stand firmly and shake both hands rapidly, increasing steadily in tempo till they are moving as fast as you can make them go.

2 The Jogger Now jog in place, increasing your tempo steadily, lifting your knees as high and as rapidly as you can.

3 The Big Flop Move in a large circular area, using as much space as available, slowly at first, with all limbs flopping loosely, like a puppet on very loose strings; be sure your whole body is completely loose—ankles, knees, hips, neck, shoulders, arms, fingers; flop along in the circular path till you feel as if you were made of rubber, or beanbags tied together, but don't fall down or stop moving till you are told to do so.

4 The Stretch-and-Shrink Now in complete contrast to No. 3, stand still and stretch as high and wide as you can. Be a tall tree as you stretch for the sky, up on your toes, pulling hard. Suddenly collapse on your heels, as small as possible, with your arms tightly pulled in, head down on knees, shrinking into atom-size. After a moment, just as suddenly, expand in all directions again, holding your place, but stretching up and out as far as you can, till you feel as if you will fly apart. Repeat the stretch/collapse sequence till you feel every muscle tingling.

Stretch

Shrink

5 The Clutching Hands Examine your hands—how they differ, how they are the same. Stretch your arms before you and, with palms outward, stretch the fingers. Now close your hands and make tight fists. Suddenly open them. Grasp an invisible rod in front of you, close your fingers around it (not crushing it, of course—keep the rod's shape intact).

6 The Climber Climb an imaginary ladder, stretching arms and hands up to the next rung, then pulling your body up, with your feet finding the rungs only long enough for balance. Climb to the top, hold on, and look down at whatever scene you see below you. Now climb back down the ladder slowly, carefully, concentrating on every muscle as you descend. Feel your arms moving out from your shoulders, your hands open, palms outward, fingers stretching and then clutching the rungs. Feel your feet pressing on the rungs, curling for balance, then releasing to move to the next rung. Climb and descend your ladder several times till you can anticipate each muscle's involvement in every

Climber on Ladder

movement. Think only of what you are doing, not how you look. Concentrate completely on the action, focus your entire being on this one pattern of movement, and think of nothing else. There is no audience—this is not a performance—no one cares what you look like. If you do it with the truth that comes from concentration, it will be right. If you don't believe it, stop doing it. Why try to fool yourself? Seek the truth in ladder-climbing, *believe* it, *do* it.

7 The Skipper Grasp the two ends of an invisible rope, test its weight, length, texture. Now use it as a jump rope and try various jumps in place. When you feel ready, and can believe it, jump rope while moving in a large circular pattern. Concentrate on your style of skipping and jumping, not on how much space you can cover, or on how you look. Keep a steady tempo and build it into smooth patterns of skipping and jumping, till you are satisfied with your skill. Be aware of all the muscles in play and enjoy using them in coordination with your patterns.

8 Yankee Doodle Gallop in a large circle while chanting or singing "Yankee Doodle" softly; as tempo increases, so does volume; clap hands to keep the rhythm and tempo going. Don't sacrifice clarity of words or cleanness of movement for speed. Concentrate on both voice and body as you increase the tempo. Think about the whole process very intently and, once the pattern is secure, let yourself enjoy it. Now continue, concentrating on the pattern, rhythm, sound of voice and hand-clapping. Enjoy it thoroughly for the freedom and swing of it.

9 The Crazy Carousel Mount an invisible merry-go-round horse, and at the signal begin slowly to move forward and up-and-down. Hold the reins loosely as the carousel gathers speed, with your knees bending and straightening but your back erect, as you move up and down on the brass pole, increasing your forward movement. Feel the shape of your wooden horse, and enjoy the wind in your face as you whirl around. Glimpse the park flashing past. The speed increases, so that you gasp for breath. The mechanics are out of control! Nothing stops your circular whirl, your rapid sliding up and down on the pole. Finally, exhausted, you fall from the horse and collapse on the floor, quite still. *Variation:* Be a robot in a mechanical routine which gradually begins to malfunction and finally goes berserk before total breakdown.

10 Now write in your own variations for any of the foregoing exercises to build an action to a state of exhaustion:

_____

_____

_____

_____

Tension and Relaxation

11 After the opening Warm-Ups, lie flat on your back, eyes closed, breathing slowly, deeply. Let your feet find relaxed angles. Be very still.

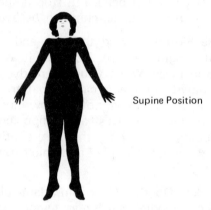

Supine Position

12 Now think about this body lying here so quietly. Think about each muscle you have used in the preceding exercises. Don't move any, just locate them in your thought. Isolate each one, mentally.

13 When you have identified each muscle, begin the tense/relax sequence. Start with your toes: spread them, tense them till each one contains power; concentrate on just the toes, hold this moment of tension, and then suddenly let go and drain all strength from the toes. Relax, then repeat the exercise. Next, the ankles: stiffen them, feel the muscles straining, hold them rigid for a moment, then relax. Repeat. The same process of tense/relax, repeated twice, will apply to the calves, knees, thighs, buttocks, spine, fingers, wrists, elbows, shoulders, neck—pressing firmly on the floor when tensing, then releasing and relaxing. When you reach the facial muscles, tighten the face into a grotesque, twisted expression, eyes closed, till every fibre is straining; hold it a moment, then relax, and repeat. Try different facial movements each time till total flexibility is achieved for mouth, jaws, cheeks, eyebrows, forehead.

SECTION TWO

WAKE-UPS

This set of exercises should help you to become aware of your senses as means of communication. Also, the faculties of concentration, imagination, and observation will gradually be sharpened with daily variations of the following routines. Again, forget the "performance complex"; you are not on stage, there is no audience, and you are not auditioning in competition. Don't waste exercise energy and concentration in talking it over with your neighbors, or in embarrassed giggling. Understand the purpose of each exercise, believe it, do it, enjoy it, and remember it.

Awakening to Awareness
(Eyes Closed)

1 Awareness Lie still and comfortably on your back on the floor, eyes closed. Relax. Be open to any ideas that may come to mind. Begin focusing your attention on specific happenings: your own inhale-exhale pattern, background sounds, the various textures you can feel all around you (but don't trace them with your hands, just be aware of them as you lie there). Become totally aware of where you are and what you are *at this moment.* Concentrate on *now.*

2 Listening Isolate these general impressions.

a   First, with eyes closed, concentrate on listening. Identify all the different sounds you can hear as you lie still. Your own breathing, of course, but then other sounds in the immediate area around you, and then in circles of space beyond. Analyze each sound, translate it into visions, shapes, colors. Immerse yourself in a private world of sounds, truly hearing for the first time, completely concentrating on the truth that each sound symbolizes for you alone.

b   Now reproduce various sounds vocally. Listen to a series of sound effects on a record and classify each sound.

c   Let one of the group start whistling a tune and someone else another tune, then a third, and so on till each one of the group is whistling his own tune—or trying to, without increasing volume.

Now try to recognize as many of your neighbors' tunes as you can, while you continue whistling your own tune!

d For an advanced exercise, enact the "listening scenes" in such plays as *The Private Ear* or *Wait Until Dark* or *The Emperor Jones*. Apply the techniques of mental isolation with eyes closed in order to concentrate fully on what you are hearing, then carry this concentration and the imagined sounds which arise into one of the scenes you wish to present. Do not attempt to impose dialogue on a "listening scene" until all your faculties for listening are in full operation. When you are finally able to listen while speaking, you will have one of these rare *total* experiences in acting.

3 Smelling Now isolate your sense of smell, inhaling slowly, carefully, to distinguish exactly each aroma that you are breathing into your nostrils.

a Identify each aroma with an adjective, such as "musty," "clean," "sharp," "choking," and so forth. Do not reject anything—savor each for its distinctness, and mentally see (through closed eyes) what each aroma signifies, at this moment.

b Try using actual smells from household items, bottle goods, flowers, grass, or food.

c Build a scene in later sessions involving aromas or perfumes (the setting could be a park, a brewery, a restaurant kitchen, a chemical plant).

d Try scenes involving both pleasant and unpleasant odors, separately or occurring simultaneously.

e Recall places you know by conjuring up their distinctive smells, and consider how this memory stimulates a sentimental emotion in you.

f For an advanced exercise, enact the "smelling scenes" from such plays as Gogol's *The Diary of a Madman* or episodes from novels or stories you've read in which odors are factors in the conflict or resolution. Your instructor may assign you to bring in such an episode and to act it out in pantomime or dramatic dialogue form. The test of your success will be the observers' awareness of what you are smelling.

4 Tasting Since it is difficult to separate smelling from tasting, examine how your mouth tastes at this moment. Be truthful with yourself.

a Now think of other places and moments with aromas and flavors. Think of how toothpaste tasted this morning, and the familiar odor of cleansing powder used in the bathroom; think of breakfast flavors, and the smell of coffee, bacon, eggs; now taste them again. Savor a special dish that you really enjoy.

b   At other sessions you can recall various places and experiences through the senses of smell and taste—some not so pleasant, some with definite memories, and some quite stimulating.

c   Can you offer any scenes from novels, stories, or plays in which tasting is important? (The men who taste water to test it for oil in the cafe scene of *The Madwoman of Chaillot*, perhaps?)

5 Touching With your eyes closed, touch and feel objects of different sizes and shapes.

a   Concentrate on different fabrics, surfaces, materials as they feel to your hands, and then to other parts of your body.

b   Relate the weight of objects to their size and shape.

c   Feel liquids of various types, some thin, others heavy like syrup.

d   Put on different types of costume pieces and feel them on your skin, such as gloves of varied materials and cuts, shoes, slippers, boots, sandals, or hats and coats.

e   Feel climate changes, heat and cold, to the point of discomfort and pain.

f   Compare pleasant with unpleasant sensations of touching: clean sheets, dirty blankets; sunshine, drizzling rain, and so forth.

g   For advanced sessions, build scenes in which you are a blind person dependent on your sense of touch. Improvise or memorize scenes from such plays as *Wait Until Dark, The Miracle Worker, Johnny Belinda.*

h   Build scenes in which the sensation from feeling different materials or temperatures is the central conflict, as in parts of *Peer Gynt* or *The Lower Depths*.

i   Build scenes to include the touch in handling a wounded arm or leg, a baby, a delicate art object.

j   As part of ensemble exercises in Part Two, include work on overcoming the fear of or reluctance to touching people by first using the touch that draws attention (tap on the shoulder, prod in the back, a well-placed kick), then the touch of comfort, or of aggression. Build scenes involving these various touches. Improvise or memorize some of the hilarious action called for in *Black Comedy*, in which the characters enact what almost amounts to a grotesque ballet as they grope their way through an apartment when the fuses are blown and cocktails are served in total darkness.

To test your powers of concentration, imagination, and observation (your "C.I.O." of improvisation), try all of these exercises first with closed eyes, to experience what is *felt* more than what is seen.

6 Now write in your own variations for awakening to awareness with closed eyes:

_____

_____

_____

_____

_____

_____

Awakening to Awareness
(Eyes Opened)

7 Resurrection Very slowly, from a totally relaxed position, let your body come alive. Gradually become aware of the ability to move again. Feel the muscles responding, the sensation of skin, of clothing, the floor beneath, all surfaces, textures. Finally, open your eyes and look straight up, while remaining supine.

8 Isolating Sight The sense of sight can be isolated in various ways. After the slow awakening, let your eyes take in at first only what is directly overhead. Examine completely what can be seen without moving your eyes—every line, form, color, and texture in that limited area. Then roll your eyes to one side and examine all that is within that range of vision; roll your eyes to the other side and repeat. These examinations must be as thorough as possible: see how lines intersect and form unsuspected patterns, or how certain colors blend or clash, or how textures vary in depth, density, or surface feeling. Can you describe in detail what you see? Are you reminded of other places and events? Are these images real or fancied? Does anything you see symbolize something else?

9 Appreciation Slowly bring yourself up to a sitting position and look around. Think about what you are seeing, concentrate on various objects, persons, colors — quite objectively, calmly, but with appreciation for the variety of sights in view. Describe everything to yourself.

10 C.I.O. Wake-Ups Many variations are possible with the basic Wake-Ups to stimulate concentration, imagination, and observation. For example:

   a Wake up to find that your hands are holding a butterfly, or some other small insect or animal. React to its touch and motion; then let it go and follow its escape with your eyes.

b Wake up to find that your hands are clasped tightly, and nothing seems to free them. Struggle in various ways to unlock them, and finally succeed after an exhausting effort.

c Wake up to find your body grotesquely twisted, with your hands clamped permanently around opposite ankles or shoulders. You cannot straighten up no matter how you try, yet like some lurching monster you must propel yourself forward on a necessary errand. When you begin to feel really entrapped by your own body, your instructor will suggest a means of release.

d Wake up to find that you are another person but with your own body and in this environment. How do you react to these now strange surroundings?

e Wake up to find that you are yourself but removed to a different place. How do you react to the unexpected change, the unfamiliar faces?

f Wake up to find yourself in someone else's body, with no knowledge of how this came about. What are your reactions?

g Wake up to find that you are another person, in another place, a different time in history.

h Wake up to find that you are yourself but enclosed in a very small, confining situation (box? casket? phone booth? pit? well? straitjacket?). Struggle to free yourself, without the aid of speech. Later, try this experience with speech, and notice the difference in impact, intensity, and truth.

Observation and Imitation

11 Living Pictures Look at a picture, photo, painting, or sketch that depicts a setting or action which you can build a scene around, using as much detail of the picture as possible. Some of the French Impressionists are excellent sources, such as Millet ("The Man with a Hoe," "The Angelus"). Members of your group may be assigned to bring in prints of portraits from different periods of history. Study some of the Dutch burgher portraits and compare them with Reynolds or Gainsborough subjects of a century later. Notice eyes, angle of head, hands, posture. Imitate these the best you can.

12 Living Machines After watching a machine in operation—such as your watch, a tape recorder, a phonograph, a floor or carpet cleaner—try to duplicate its movements; then build this into a robot scene. There are several plays from which you can extract ideas for mechanized humans, and in advanced sessions you might present these scenes for evaluation. Consider *The Hairy Ape, The Adding Machine, 1984, R.U.R., Saturday Night and Sunday Morning.*

Living Machines

13 Actual versus Imagined Objects Combine the senses of sight and touch in scenes, working with your partner in common actions such as smoking, having tea or coffee, dining together. Use actual objects first, then imagined ones, concentrating on such visual aspects as size, shape, texture, and color.

14 Occupation Imitations Concentrate your attention on occupations of people using things, and build what you observe into scenes: gas station attendants, plumbers, cooks, barbers and beauticians, and so forth. This exercise will involve some outside preparation. Perhaps your instructor will want you to hand in a written account of your observations with a note of the length of time you spent. If so, you would need to record such details as age, physical appearance, clothing and accessories, mannerisms, voice qualities, speech patterns, traits, and attitudes, as well as the actions and reactions of the people being observed. An ideal location would be a restaurant or coffee shop where the manager would not mind your sitting in a corner and taking notes quietly and unobtrusively. You may confine your observation notes to just one person, but your instructor can determine the extent of details for the assignment. Later, in Part Three you will see how this exercise is basic to Act-Ups 1-*b*.

15 Isolated Features Concentrate your observation on one area of your body at a time—such as hands and arms, feet and legs—so as to appreciate their expressiveness in building scenes.

16 Life Cycle Perhaps one of the most interesting Wake-Ups for an advanced group is the Life Cycle (also a Move-Up exercise). Wake up as a newborn child and develop in successive stages from infancy (helplessness, the mysteries of hands and feet, grasping, crawling, finally standing only to fall) to childhood (toddling, walking, running, skipping, hopping), to youth (striding, marching, dancing, skating, and other athletic movements), to maturity (strolling, efficient movements, job routines, domestic routines, mannerisms), to old age (slow tempo, stiffness, careful movements, handicaps), to death (extreme difficulty in movement, frailness, brittleness, helplessness, collapse, inertia, expiration). Each of these stages should be mentally weighed first, and neither dramatized nor combined with another person in any way; speech is irrelevant at this point, since this is an extreme application of the physical senses and body to communication. But the truth of each movement, each action and reaction, must be tested and accepted by the individual doing it, or else the exercise has no meaning. When you feel ready for this one, try it; you may be surprised at its effect on your approach to the whole art of acting.

17 Now write in your own variations for any of the foregoing exercises for Observation and Imitation:

_____

_____

_____

_____

_____

SECTION THREE

MOVE-UPS

With your less inhibited body to work with, the following daily exercises or their equivalents will help you coordinate your mind and body in recognizable activities. Remember, your exercises in spontaneous movement will not be criticized or judged, since at this stage of development your primary objective is to seek the truth of each gesture, each action, and your secondary objective is to execute each gesture and action with truth. *Believe* it, then *do* it *believably.*

1 Circle Walks Stand with the group in as large a circle as the area permits, all facing in one direction. While walking round the perimeter of the circle, respond to directions immediately as they are given. *Think with your body.*

a Walk freely, openly, tall.

b Walk through mud, deep and sticky, first in shoes, then barefooted.

c Walk in the desert, through brush and cacti with many prickles and stickers.

d Walk barefoot on hot burning sand.

e Walk in the soft, wet sand near the water's edge.

f Walk barefoot along the ocean's edge in cool, ebbing and flowing water.

g Walk on the rocks near the water, slippery and slimy, with crabs, too!

h Walk as best you can through the nearest waves, then out a bit to deeper water. (Watch out for currents!)

i Walk through autumn leaves, dry and brittle underfoot; watch them fall, and try to catch them.

j Walk along tossing a ball and catching it, quite casually.

k Walk in a lonely place late at night; hear something behind you but go on.

l Walk into a forest, thick with brambles and low branches, but push on.

m Walk in outer space, weightless, slowly turning as you move along.

n   Walk in a dream, attempting to reach someone but never quite getting there.

o   Walk in a nightmare, trying to escape something horrible, but in slow motion.

2   Jog-and-Freeze   Again stand in a circle, all facing in one direction. Be free in movement and open-minded for this one. Spontaneity is the key, and any preplanning or anticipation will destroy the purpose. Your body position is going to dictate your thought for this exercise, rather than the usual process of thought-then-action. Here are the basic steps—you can add your own variations later:

a   Jog around the circle at medium-fast tempo. Stop instantly on command. Freeze. When asked, describe what position you are frozen in, or let others tell you what they think your position suggests.

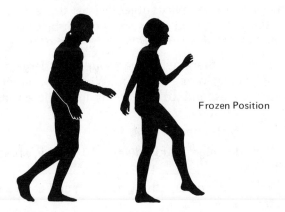

Frozen Position

b   *Variation:* From frozen position, develop a piece of action including the preparation (that is, tensing up in anticipation of making a gesture or movement), the stroke (the actual movement or gesture), and the follow-through (the sustained pose after completing an action, as in baseball pitching). Allow an emotion to motivate your action, or, conversely, allow your action to arouse an emotion.

c   *Variation:* Develop a short scene with a partner to include your frozen position as the climax tableau, or curtain-action.

d   *Variation:* Write in your own Jog-and-Freeze exercises:

_____

_____

_____

_____

3 Balloons-and-Dreams Stand in a circle, facing center. A real balloon will be used and then removed so that you can recreate your handling of it exactly, without any object. This will test your concentration and observation abilities to the utmost, and finally lead into an application of imagination as well. This is also a good early ensemble exercise.

> **a**   A balloon is tossed to one person in the circle, who lightly strikes it toward the next, moving the balloon around the circle. When all have received and passed it along, the balloon is removed, and the whole routine is redone with an invisible balloon, testing everyone's powers of concentration and observation. Each gesture, action, and reaction must be recreated as nearly as possible.

> **b**   The balloon is tossed up in the center of the circle and batted about from one person to another, to keep it aloft, but with no set pattern. Repeat the exercise exactly without the balloon.

> **c**   The balloon is tossed into the group, but in slow motion; all respond with dreamlike slow movements to keep the balloon moving about the group. Remove the balloon and repeat the exercise in slow motion.

> **d**   From the slow-motion experiment develop a dramatic situation, as in a dream. For advanced sessions, background music may help.

4 Listen-and-Move Sit anywhere in the area where you are isolated from anyone else, with lighting very dim. Do not move until you can believe completely in what you feel. If you don't believe it, don't do it. Sit and wait.

> **a**   Listen to a recording of classical music, concentrate on what it is saying, imagine yourself in motion to the music, and then let yourself be drawn naturally to interpret the music physically. This is not a dance lesson, only an experiment in spontaneous response of the body to serious music.

> **b**   Repeat the exercise, but with avant-garde orchestral music; or with serious jazz (Gershwin, Kenton, Thompson) or electronic or rock arrangements, but not for dance interpretation. Just patterns of free movement.

> **c**   Repeat the exercise, but use sound-effects recordings, or drums, or electronic music for extremely weird sounds.

5 Hands-and-Face Sitting in front of a table mirror, you are going to get very acquainted with your physical image, first your hands, then your face.

> **a**   Look at both your hands carefully, and then at their reflection in the mirror. Be able to describe your hands thoroughly to yourself, then to a partner. Do not look at your hands when you are offering the description.

b   Give life to your hands as animate beings in themselves. Stage a scene in the mirror with them as if they were puppets.

c   Using the back of the mirror as the puppet stage, stand behind it (on the glass side) and present a scene for your partner with your hands as actors. Then it's the partner's turn to give "handsies"

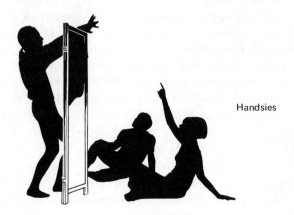

Handsies

scenes for you. Perhaps some of these scenes will be presented to the whole group, with partners possibly combining their "casts" for a joint scene. Such a performance can be given from behind a screen that conceals all but the hands. A musical recording might provide accompaniment; but it would take some outside preparation, and the emphasis in this exercise is on imagination as well as fun.

d   Now your face: study it carefully in the mirror. Move every facial muscle until you are familiar with the range and extent of mobility.

e   From the blankest expressions, run the gamut of moods which your face can convey. Try each mood warily, with subtle restraint, and gradually intensify the expression into an exaggerated mask, then return gradually to blankness.

f   Interpret various characters with your face, from a plain person to a beautiful or handsome model to a hideous monster. Try different ages in the same way.

g   Now with your partner, test each other's ability to communicate, using first the hands only, then facial expressions only, and finally both hands and face. Let the observer describe the message aloud as it is being delivered. Then after the solo testings, enter into a lively conversation between yourselves, using only hands and face, no vocal sounds. Try switching partners with other teams for more objectivity.

(At this point it may be interesting to discuss the Theatre of the Deaf and some of the articles about their tours which may be found by using the *Readers' Guide to Periodical Literature.*)

h To apply concentration to your expressive hands and face, select an everyday task or occupation and perform it for truth in every detail. Use no real objects but depend on memory of observation.

i Use a mask to conceal your face, or put over your head a paper bag or cloth with eye and nose openings. Now establish a character for type and age, letting your body and hands do all the work. Then uncover your face and repeat the same action. Discuss the feelings and values you experience from this. It is possible to develop scenes in which masked ones are in the minority, or the majority, so that group prejudices can be dramatically enacted.

j With your partner, do a double-image whereby one stands behind the other and extends his arms down to the elbows close to the sides of the front partner, who has pulled his arms back and clasped them behind him. The front partner does the talking, while the back partner gestures appropriately. It may help for the back person to press his head against the shoulders of the front person in order to feel the voice vibrations and thus to respond with more immediate gestures.

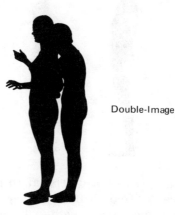

Double-Image

A few practice sessions in front of a mirror will be hilarious but helpful. It is a good idea to let the speaker describe a specific

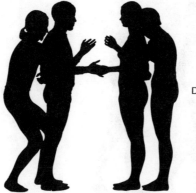

Double-Images

object—how to use it, play it, or make it—while the hands partner holds it, points out its features, and generally complements what is being said. This exercise may or may not prove that two heads are better than one, but it certainly will develop concentration, observation, and imagination. Later, conversations and scenes may be staged with double-images of two or more teams.

6 Stage Movement The purpose in the following exercises is to develop the best "normal image" for stage and offstage poise and posture. Any basic book on acting techniques may be used for specific instructions and exercises, but be sure to cover each of the following with a coach:

a *Standing posture:* well-balanced, erect, confident, poised, relaxed. Hold this position for a long time, while instructions are given on other matters. Use a full-length mirror for observation and concentration. Be aware of temptations to break the poise by extraneous movements.

Good Posture for Normal Standing

b *Walking posture:* relaxed to permit freedom of muscles; firm abdomen, lifted diaphragm; legs swinging easily from the hips, bending the knees, with a balance-and-push-off sequence, easy stride length; shoulders steady, head high, all movement from the waist down, stepping lightly, but firmly.

Good Posture for Normal Walking

c *Turns:* pivot on the balls of the feet, shifting weight to other leg on completion; pivot in opposite direction and shift weight, doing both quarter- and half-turns in place, then walking turns.

d *Varied walks:* strolling, pacing, hurrying, running, tiptoeing; upstairs, downstairs.

e *Varied postures:* stooping, picking up something from the floor, kneeling, sitting, rising, perching on an edge (table, wall, armrest), lying down, sitting and lying on the floor. Try sitting on a chair in as many positions as you can. Expand this into standing or kneeling on the chair to depict all the moods and attitudes you can think of. Learn to use furniture for expressing feelings through bodily postures.

f *Falling:* fainting—into a chair, onto a couch, into someone's arms, or directly to the floor (falling to either side, forward or backward, from a standing position); recovering from faint; falling when stabbed, shot, or struck from standing and sitting positions, directly to floor, or onto couch, or downstairs; straight falls downstairs, or off a chair; and comedy falls, sprawls, stumbling, bumping, tripping.

g Try each of these basic postures and movements in terms of characters of particular types and ages. Seek the truth in each variation. Believe in the reality of the character to convey the reality of his body.

h The Life Cycle (see Wake-Up, p. 14); Finally, live a complete life, from newborn infancy to childhood, youth, maturity, middle age, old age, and death—in silent movements, true for each age. Concentrate on what you have observed, and your imagination will lead you to depict each action with sensitivity and truth.

7 Object Responses Now imagination and concentration come into full use as you coordinate the senses, especially seeing and touching, as well as proper movement to convey a specific reaction to what you see and touch. Your sequence is (*a*) experiencing, (*b*) reproducing or describing the experience, (*c*) relating the experience in free association or as a link in a series, and (*d*) using the results in a scene. In other words, you go from observation of real things and people (your experience), to discovering further uses of the actual and imagined elements (reproducing or describing your experience), to creating something new from your imagination based on your insight into the actual experience (free association and linking into a series), and finally realizing the unlimited scope of your imagination (applied in a scene or series of scenes). Start simply and gradually involve more complicated experiences.

a Look at and handle a familiar object; then remove the object and handle it in your imagination. Do this with a tool or such apparatus as a record player. First the real, then your imagined action.

b   Watch someone skipping rope, looking for something in pockets or bag, performing some constructive action; then perform the same actions accurately with imaginary objects. Your partner may help on this one, alternating roles with you.

c   Describe to your partner where a real object is to be found somewhere nearby; then test your descriptive ability by letting your partner find it.

d   Look at a filmstrip or series of slides; then recall the order and content of each frame, seeing it clearly in imagination. This exercise may well be coupled with a demonstration lesson on makeup, blocking, or the like.

e   Listen to a recording of sound effects, then recall each in imagination, first immediately after listening to the sound, then when some other sound has occurred between the first item listened to and your recollection of it.

f   Drink a small quantity of fruit juice or other tasteful beverage and try to recall the exact taste in imagination. This can be done on your own at any meal. Also, smell some mint or other herb, and recall it in imagination.

g   Place a chair in the center of the group, and respond to it, as you see it in imagination, in different positions—on its side, upside down—or as something else entirely, such as a barrier, a hovel, an instrument.

h   Treat any of the following as something else: a shoe, book, pen, ring. Try to find as many ways of using each as possible. Then remove the object and work without it.

i   Reversing the process, imagine an object, maybe a tool or an appliance. Use it realistically in imagination; then give it an added dimension that enlarges its use to a fanciful extreme—perhaps it talks, or ignites, or takes on human attributes. Imagine, for example, that clothing takes on the characteristics of the wearer. Next develop a tension, a conflict, and build into a scene.

j   Wake up to find a real, unidentified object on your chest, while your eyes remain closed. Discover what the object is by touch, then open your eyes, and use it. Repeat the experience without the object, in imagination.

k   Another Wake-Up combining principles of Object Response is to waken underneath a drape or curtain which completely covers you, as in a cocoon. Let your imagination place you in a circumstance where this might occur, and react accordingly. Or awake under the curtain and let it become a garment representative of some type of character: a classic Roman toga, a spy's cloak, a laundered sheet, a royal robe, a straitjacket, a tent, a witch's cape. With each awakening, be someone else responding to the drapery. Later, using speech, rise with the garment clothing you in a specific emotion (love, hate, fear) and react to a partner or with the whole group.

l   Your small group is given one object, to which you must respond with the group and build a scene involving the object as the key to conflict. There must be no preplanning, for spontaneity is the test.

m   Spontaneous chain reactions occur when a real object is passed around the whole group; then an unseen object is passed around to elicit reactions.

n   For more spontaneous application of concentration and imagination, let an object be placed in view on a table or in a jacket pocket. Your partner tries to take this object while distracting your concentration, and you attempt the same with him.

o   Try the same exercise, using a hat, which each in turn tries to snatch off the other's head and wear himself, while you both keep up a sensible conversation.

p   Working first in solo, then in pairs, and later in trios, start inventing something practical and let it develop into as many other things as you can, each thing growing out of the previous one, in a series of spontaneous transformations. For example, suppose you and your partner invent (in pantomime) an all-purpose brush, for hair, clothing, shoes, floors, and the like. In the midst of sharing it for all sorts of tasks, one of you suddenly fastens a long handle to it and it becomes a broom; then another turns it into a pogo stick, then a shovel, a rake, and so on. This may seem challenging enough for two, but try it with three persons, or four, a different person changing the item each time around and the others using it his way before someone changes it again. The faster the changes, the more exciting it is, but each change should be executed by all the users before the next one occurs.

q   Now write in your own variations for any of the foregoing exercises demonstrating responses to objects.

_____

_____

_____

_____

_____

_____

SECTION FOUR

SPEAK-UPS

The importance of stage speech cannot be stressed too much. That this technique occurs at this advanced point in our sequence does not minimize it but rather means to focus it as a climactic part of daily drill. Many excellent texts on stage speech are available and may be consulted for specific disciplines of voice and diction. In the improvisational process, however, we are concerned primarily with encouraging spontaneous speech of relevance, rightness, and clarity. Later, some exercises may be added for drill on particular problems of dialect, projection, and variety. Even though speech may have been used spontaneously in previous exercises, it now becomes central to scene-building. As usual, exercises start in gamelike simplicity and work into complex patterns.

1 Touch-and-Go All lie supine on the floor, eyes closed, feet to center of the circle, touching neighbors' little toes and little fingers. You feel the unity of the circle, and you are aware of your neighbors to right and left. Think about it in silence for a few moments.

a On a signal, one person makes a vocal sound of some sort, his neighbor to the right imitates it, and then *his* neighbor to the right repeats the sound exactly as he just heard it, not as it sounded from the first person. This continues around the circle, each one imitating the sound that comes from the left, passing it to the one on the right, until it reaches the one who started it—and who may no longer recognize it. Concentration and observation!

b *Variations:* Instead of a mere vocal sound, use in order: a nonsense syllable, a word, a phrase, a sentence, a statement. You will progress in both listening and imitative skills. Spontaneous group reaction will indicate your success or failure, and no further comment will be needed at this time.

2 Word Association Join a small group of three or four and sit facing one another in a tight circle. You are now going to build vocal continuity by listening and responding.

a Using a simple stream-of-consciousness technique, let one person say a word to which another person responds immediately with another word, and continue several times around the circle, responding each time to whatever word has just been said.

b   Instead of a single word, let the starter speak a sentence, and you reply in turn with another sentence, building an idea of consistency and meaning.

3 Storytelling   Retain the small groups or subdivide into pairs.

a   Let the starter begin a narrative, a story, that will include exposition of place, time, or characters, but mention only one of these. Each speaker in turn adds another element, another dimension, and of course a conflict, until a speaker uses one of his turns to resolve the conflict and end the story. It might be you! Keep your contributions very brief so that the circle may be encompassed numerous times during the interval allowed for this exercise. It will be wise to put a time limit on these exercises, by the way, or else the purpose of concentration and meaningful speech will be lost. Watch out for the temptation in yourself to limit the group's spontaneity by consistently returning to a self-determined pattern of development despite the contributions of others. This would reveal personal limitations in listening and imagination.

b   *Variation:*   In a group of four or five, when you have made your contribution to the story, ask the next speaker "how" or "when" or "why" or "where" so that he must build on that question with his contribution. Then he in turn concludes with such a one-word question to his neighbor, and so on.

c   *Variation:*   Subdivide all present into small groups of three or more. When all groups are underway with their respective stories, have the instructor switch individuals among the groups. This will test you for concentration and imagination, for when you join another group midway in their story, you have to forget the story you have just left and pick up the new one immediately. By the end of the exercise, no one should be in the group he started with, and each one might have been switched several times. A general recapitulation afterwards will reveal how each story developed and ended. This exercise is also effective in illustrating ensemble attitudes.

d   *Variation:*   The starter puts an imaginary object inside an invisible suitcase as he describes it; the next one takes out and describes quite a different object, and gives it to a third person, who packs something else, and so on. Each one alternates packing or removing an object, but the point is that each object suggests the next response. This can become quite complicated and depends on your utmost observation, imagination, and concentration. The starter eventually closes the suitcase and leaves on his trip when he feels all packed.

e   Now write in your original variations on the foregoing exercises of Word Associations to develop memory as well as ensemble disciplines:

_____

_____

_____

_____

_____

4 Famous Voices These exercises may require some research and practice, but they provide an interesting discipline and meaningful stimuli to further discussions not only on speech techniques but also on the ideas presented.

a   Select a passage from the biography or autobiography of a famous actor or actress and read it aloud to everyone or to a smaller group. Try to assume the attitude of the writer at the time of the writing, as if it were a letter or a bit of conversation. The listeners may comment on your vocal interpretation of this selection. Next, present a no-script, improvised version of the passage, including the same ideas in your own words, yet retaining the style and feeling of the original. This will take repeated efforts but will reveal your understanding of the words, as well as the empathy necessary to interpret them sensitively and sincerely. You may surprise yourself and others with some very pleasing results.

b   Using recordings of plays, imitate certain speeches by famous actors or actresses. Where two tape recorders are available, use the first to play the professional version, picking it up on the second machine; then stop the first tape and go ahead with your imitation of it on the second one. Play back your tape to hear both versions, and study closely every intonation, pronunciation, modulation, and so forth. When you think you can imitate the famous voice expertly, tape yourself again, and then follow immediately with the professional. The playback may be disappointing, or amusing, or encouraging. At any rate, it is surprising how much progress in good speech style can start with these self-help imitations of famous models.

Of course, it would be pointless and limiting to continue imitating a model after you have discovered your own speech style. For improvisational application of what you learn in these taping sessions, try using your model's voice and speech mannerisms in ordinary conversation with a partner. Test yourself for observation and concentration, as well as consistency, sincerity, and truthful identity with the original. Don't succumb to the temptation to do extreme characterizations of stereotypes, such as "party imitations" of well-known movie personalities.

5 Diction Drills For general improvement in pronunciation, follow the two-tape procedure in imitating a professional recording of speech drills. This process works for foreign dialect drills as well as for standard American. However, you should handle individual speech problems or styles as a separate lesson, apart from regular stage speech. Affecting any speech mannerisms will certainly limit your effort to achieve a versatile acting style based on the principle of improvisation: to seek the truth.

a   Guide sheets for diction and vocal quality drills are available and you may use them for private as well as group study, with or without a tape recorder.

b   You and a partner might actually telephone each other at home in a pre-arranged time sequence and test abilities to be understood while conveying preplanned emotional moods: anger, impatience, affection, worry, and the like. These calls are more effective when brief—two or three minutes—but intensely sincere. How does emotion affect *your* diction?

Ask Yourself

After a number of sessions have included some exercises from each of the units in Part One (Warm-Ups, Wake-Ups, Move-Ups, and Speak-Ups), test your progress with the questions listed below and any other that may have occurred to you. Space is allowed for written answers, in case you wish to submit these to your instructor for further advice on your C.I.O. (Concentration—Imagination—Observation).

Concentration

1 Do I understand the contrast between tension and relaxation?

2 Can I identify the major muscles of my body and face which are used in conveying ideas?

3 Is my body more expressive of moods, attitudes, and ideas than it was?

4 Can I make my body respond to every prevailing thought and condition?

5 Has my body become more poised, graceful, and confident in both standing and sitting postures?

6 Can I walk in a normal manner, with relaxed grace, while making myself as tall as possible?

7 Can I shift my weight to allow balance when turning or when changing direction in walking?

8 Have my hands grown more expressive, more communicative, more interesting?

9 Can I handle objects with more assurance, poise, and dexterity than I used to?

10 Can I carry on a conversation with a partner while engaged in a pantomime bit of business such as pouring and drinking a beverage, eating, or making something?

11 Can I coordinate body and voice in rhythmic exercises?

12 Am I making an effort to overcome lazy speech habits by regularly drilling on enunciation, articulation, and proper word pronunciation for syllabication and stress?

13 Am I practicing proper breathing for speech and projection, and working to place my voice at a comfortable pitch, with resonance and richness in tone?

14 Have I become more familiar with theories of acting as voiced by different actors in published and recorded materials?

Signed _____

Date _____

Imagination

1 Am I developing my imaginative powers?

2 Can I walk in a variety of ways through a variety of situations, instantly believing each one to the point of experiencing appropriate physical sensations?

3 Can I develop a specific physical attitude or posture into a believable scene, with that attitude as the key image or climactic moment?

4 Can I respond physically to unfamiliar music or sound effects so that my body conveys my impressions of what I hear?

5 Can I use a chair in assuming all sorts of attitudes, characters, and ages as I sit or lean or stand on it?

6 Am I so familiar with my hands that they can become entities in themselves?

7 Am I so familiar with my face that I can make it express an assortment of ages, moods, or ideas?

8 Can my feet, like my hands, be expressive in conveying attitudes and moods?

9 Can I handle unseen objects in pantomime with economy of movement, yet project specific images and ideas? Does the unseen object retain its reality?

10 Is my imagination active enough that I can turn an object into another object in just my handling of it?

11 Is my imagination vivid enough that I can adapt to a developing idea as it unfolds in group storytelling, rather than monopolize or distort the theme to my own preference?

12 Am I able to separate myself from the actual environment and project myself into an imagined one?

13 Am I able to imagine myself in the physical shape of a quite different person, reacting and adjusting to the actual location where I am at the moment?

14 Can I imagine an environment so foreign to my sense of freedom or well-being that I react with physical tension and mental anguish?

Signed _____

Date _____

Observation

1 Am I learning how to observe people, places, and things as creative stimuli?

2 Is my personal life becoming enriched through wider awareness of the world around me?

3 Can I identify and even imitate most sounds I hear?

4 Can I identify and describe in detail various aromas, flavors? Can I recall any of these for immediate use in a scene?

5 Can I identify and describe in detail various surfaces, materials, textures? Can I recall any of these for immediate use in a scene?

6 Am I more observant than I was of details of color, line, pattern? Can I concentrate fully on one spot within my vision and recreate it mentally when not actually seeing it?

7 Can I recreate any simple movement of a person or a mechanical object?

8 Can I bring to life a still painting or photo by assuming physical characteristics of the central figures?

9 Do I understand the physical characteristics of each of the ages of man, and can I depict them believably? Do I actually believe their reality while enacting them?

10 Do I have one or more models of excellent stage speech to follow in developing my own style of speaking?

11 Do I appreciate the subtleties used by professional actors in their pitch, inflectional variety, tone, volume, rhythm, and tempo?

12 Do I hear dialect differences, and can I imitate some of these as used in theatre?

Signed _____

Date _____

Ask Your Instructor

You and your group members may feel the need for open discussions with your instructor from time to time. The application of some of the experiences to acting techniques may not be immediately clear; or you may want more detailed explanation of specific strengths and weaknesses you have observed in yourself or others. In order to channel spontaneous and fragmented discussion into constructive evaluations, here are a few questions to get you started. No doubt you will have many more that need asking.

1   Am I (are we) becoming more imaginative and spontaneous in conveying impressions?

2   Do I (do we) seem to be fully concentrating when engaged in creative activity?

3   Do I (do we) seem to be replacing inhibitions with creative awareness?

4   Am I (are we) employing all the physical senses to convey specific impressions to you?

5   Do I (do we) appear to you to be more relaxed while engaged in creative action?

6   What strengths have you noted that might give trouble if not disciplined soon?

7   What strengths have you noted that will be most helpful in later characterizations?

8   What weaknesses have you seen that need immediate attention?

9   What weaknesses have you seen that will need considerable time and experience to overcome?

10   What indications show us to be ready for Ensemble Exercises?

Part Two

Ensemble Exercises

Following a selection of Daily Exercises at each session to rouse your C.I.O., you should be ready for group work. Of course, in Part One you have encountered a few partner, small group, or whole group exercises, but their benefit has been mostly personal. Now we shall stress interaction for greater truth in reaction. That is what acting really is: action that leads to *re*-action. It is best achieved when all participants accept the result as a group effort rather than as a series of solos.

The following exercises should help you to—

- Apply the principles of the Daily Exercises in group situations.
- Integrate your individuality into a creative group effort.
- Accept contributions of others by minimizing *self*-consciousness.
- Listen and observe so that your action develops from reaction.
- Appreciate the harmonious artistry of ensemble timing, tempo, and truth.

SECTION FIVE

GROUP-UPS

Focus now on the ensemble attitude: scene-sharing, spotlight-shifting according to developing action, and timing.

1 Silent Mirrors This exercise will help you to apply the technique of observation when working with one or more persons in a scene.

a Share a table mirror with a partner and imitate each other's facial expressions, attempting first the stereotyped emotions but gradually becoming more subtle and sincere. Remove the mirror and take turns being actor and image.

b Stand facing your partner and alternate as actor and mirror image, starting with very simple movements, slow and clear, to permit exact duplications. Gradually become more complex, with more natural tempo, with unexpected variations.

Mirror Image

c Increase the number of "mirrors" by lining up in single file, diagonally, so that each "image" can clearly see the actor, who faces the line of "mirrors" and does such a familiar action as washing hands, shaving, or applying makeup.

Mirror Lineup

d Build a silent scene around a mirror, such as in a barbershop, hairdresser's, theatre dressing room, or store selling hats, ties. After your small ensemble performs a scene successfully, you may wish to present it for comment from the whole group.

e For advanced sessions, you may wish to do a "mirror scene" from a well-known play. In Act I of Elmer Rice's *Dream Girl,* Georgia carries on a conversation with herself as she sits at her dressing table, while Laudisi in Pirandello's *It Is So If You Think So* (or *Right You Are If You Think You Are*) opens a scene in conversation with his mirror image. Your group may recall other plays in which action centers briefly on a mirror. Don't forget the wicked queen in *Snow White,* or the vain monarch in *The Emperor's New Clothes.*

2 Sound-Track Scenes Now your observation technique must include such total absorption that you can anticipate what your image or counterpart will say, so that a synchronization can occur.

a With three or four others, you are silent screen actors in a scene while your counterparts provide voices from the sidelines, virtually a lip-synchronized sound track. Reverse roles and repeat. This requires utmost concentration and observation by the voices to anticipate the actors' movements and responses, which should be at a controlled tempo until the voices adjust to the situation. Let the plot and characters be very familiar, even sterotyped, while experimenting.

b For advanced sessions, more subtle and complex scenes can be tried. Perhaps you can even vocalize sound effects for the later experiments. Try for some heavy dramatic conflict, as well as for light farce or high comedy situations.

Sound Track

3 Shadow-Conscience This exercise will force you to be aware of the others in the ensemble as well as of yourself. No more than four persons should work together on this one.

a Two sets of partners are needed. Two people engage in conversation, but each has a Conscience who shadows him so closely that observers cannot see or hear the Conscience whispering suggestions and responses to the Speaker. The problem is harder when the Speaker tries to reject his Conscience and to reply with comments quite opposite to those of the "still, small voice." It is best if the Conscience always keeps his face close to the upstage ear of the Speaker. Suggestions for situations occur in your daily life: housewife and door-to-door salesman or promotor; teacher and parent, teacher and student, parent and child. Conflict subject matter can be simple or profound, so long as Speakers can respond positively or negatively to their respective Consciences. It is easy to see how this exercise will develop an ability to recognize "sub-text" when learning dialogue in script rehearsals.

b *Variation*: Replace the Conscience with a Devil-Voice for one or both Speakers, and see how the scene develops. Speakers should be imaginary characters but in a realistic setting and situation. The simpler the truer.

c Let Shadows and Speakers switch roles. Remember that these scenes are not suitable for audience performances, since only the Speaker hears his Shadow.

d For later sessions, or even for public performance, it may be possible to present an improvisation in which the Shadow Voice, whether Conscience or Devil, is projected over a P.A. system, so that all can hear what the Shadow is whispering to the Speaker. Of course, the timing would have to be good to avoid excessive voice-overlapping among the Speakers and their Shadows. However, with a little experimenting it might prove quite exciting. In fact, it may be possible to use this approach in presenting a scene from a well-known play. Think of the possibilities in the encounter of the two young ladies in *The Importance of Being Earnest,* or between Billy and Claggart in *Billy Budd* or between Hamlet and Polonius in *Hamlet.* As Mark Twain once said, "Words were invented to conceal our thoughts," and this exercise may prove how right he was.

Shadow-Conscience

4 Touch-and-Go-Go This exercise with its variations is intended to help overcome any inhibitions you might have in establishing physical contact with another performer in a scene.

a   With your partner, touching only fingertips, start a rhythmic movement, perhaps to music or a drumbeat, never losing touch with your fingertips.

Fingertips Touching

b   In the same manner, try the movement touching only toes.

Toes Touching

c In the same manner, try the movement touching only right or left shoulders.

Shoulders Touching

d Join others and form a circle, again touching only one small part of the body (such as fingertips, toes, or shoulders) and move *together* in rhythm. If a complicated maneuver develops, all must follow, keeping in touch no matter what happens. A feeling of mutual dependence usually results.

Group Touching

e   Continue this exercise, but at a given signal break the physical touch while remaining aware of and responsive to the others as you move separately yet together. This takes keen observation, concentration, and anticipation.

Group Contact

f   The balloon of Daily Exercise Move-Ups Exercise 3, p. 19, may be used again at this point to review interplay in movement, perhaps with musical accompaniment.

g   Review Wake-Ups 5-*j*, p. 11, at this point and expand into scenes from well-known plays requiring ·physical contact such as fighting or embracing or caressing. Your instructor and any good acting textbook will offer suggestions on stage positions and timing for such action.

5 Touch-and-See   This exercise enlarges on Wake-Ups 13 and 14, p. 14, to include ensemble techniques of working with partners and props.

a   You and your partner become engrossed in handling various objects—tableware, drinks, coffee or tea service—with much handing back and forth. After using actual objects, repeat the same scene with imaginary ones. The accent here is on interplay and reaction to your partner's involvement with the objects, as well as your own contribution to the action. Let spontaneity result from ensemble imagination so that you build creatively and truthfully. Scenes from plays often include table action, such as eating in *Ah, Wilderness!, The Petrified Forest, A View from the Bridge, The Matchmaker,* or *Tom Jones.* Well-timed business of eating or serving can help to emphasize certain key words or lines so that the action is an accompaniment and not just an interesting diversion for the dialogue.

b   Become involved with your partner, or several people, in some busy occupation familiar to you all: a mechanical repair, a clean-up job, any creative or domestic task. When ready, try the housecleaning scene from *A Raisin in the Sun,* or an excerpt from some other play involving group action with props.

c   You join everybody in watching some imaginary sight: an airplane, a cloud, a construction crane. After the ensemble attitude has evolved, build a scene involving the whole group which starts with one or two individuals seeing something dramatic (person on the ledge of a high building, an airplane in trouble, a ship in distress), and gradually a crowd gathers. Keep your speech to a minimum, stressing tense observation through complete physical and mental concentration. (When danger is seen, crowds generally huddle together for reassurance.) You won't feel like being a soloist if you help the whole group experience a unity in the truth you and they create together. One of the most well-known "crowd-watching" scenes in recent theatre has been the "Racetrack Scene" in *My Fair Lady*, which requires complete discipline on the part of the singing chorus as they work together to create the impression of seeing the race start, being run, and end at the finish line.

d   A variation on group-watching is the group-listening exercise: a strange sound is heard by one, then another, and another until all of you are listening intently, afraid to speak, but trying to communicate to each other your respective curiosities, doubts, and finally fears or adjustments. But whatever the final reaction, it must be the same for all. Such old plays as *Seven Keys to Baldpate,* or *Seven Little Indians* or other "haunted-house" type settings, offer group-listening suspense scenes.

6 Hear-and-Speak   This exercise will help you to keep cool and poised regardless of interruptions or upsetting circumstances while you are playing a scene. It also introduces the conflict of emotions which characters often must project, with one attitude being dominant.

a   Read a newspaper article aloud as others try to interrupt your concentration.

b   Read a short story aloud while others interrupt you. When they do, put your finger at the place where you stop, listen to the interrupter politely, make a logical reply, calmly but firmly, then continue reading aloud until the next interruption, as a test of concentration on continuity. It will help if you have practiced reading the story aloud before attempting this exercise.

c   Deliver a speech on an important subject, while several hecklers try to upset you; hold to your argument without losing your composure in any way. The hecklers should base their interruptions on your speech, not on you as a person, but you always return to your line of reasoning after calmly replying to their comments. You might even succeed in silencing them by your confidence and logic. On the other hand, the incident may build into chaos.

d   Build a scene in which an official representing an institution is confronted with protestors. Ideas are readily found in the daily news. Act IV of Ibsen's *An Enemy of the People* is the town meeting scene, in which a doctor stands alone against the community on a grave moral issue.

e Build a scene in which a famous public figure, a hero to the masses, meets his doting fans. Again, daily news items provide actual situations. A famous one in recent theatre was in *Bye Bye, Birdie,* the musical about a teen-age singing star.

7 Gibberish Contemporary theatre, as well as the movement called Absurdism, have produced many plays in which intentionally meaningless dialogue is used to point up man's inability to communicate through mere words. For example, Ionesco uses this technique in *The Bald Soprano* and *The Lesson.* Often grunts and groans, as well as nonsense syllables, are used by playwrights to indicate feelings rather than ideas. Refer to such a masterpiece of Absurdism as *Waiting for Godot,* which includes several such moments. This exercise in gibberish will help you experience such techniques, and may add to your range of communication devices onstage.

a Experiment with creating foreign-sounding language out of nonsense syllables. Do not attempt to incorporate sounds or inflections from languages you may be familiar with. Concentrate instead on conveying meaning through inflection, emphasis, and timing. You will really have to be thinking in English of what you are saying, while speaking your thoughts in meaningless sounds. Gestures will help to some extent, but as spontaneous expressions, not as sign language. Try it with a partner.

b Now in gibberish show a small group the merits of some article—a chair, a garment, or such. Try using the style of a product demonstrator at a fair: smooth handling of tools or various objects, while pouring out a nonstop commentary. Notice how the television car salesmen handle their microphones, signboards, and maps without taking their eyes off the camera. They are inevitable subjects for satire, but their techniques are expertly hypnotic.

c Be a gibberish salesperson and demonstrate a product, a new garment, a new idea, to a large group, who will ask questions in English as they attempt to understand you. Then repeat the exercise with *everyone* speaking gibberish. You may be surpised how well communication takes place through clear intonation and gesture and the various emphasis devices that you will acquire.

d Build a scene in which you plead seriously in gibberish for another's favor or understanding. Develop the situation into two groups, one pleading and one responding, alternating English and gibberish between them.

e Test yourself for continuity by switching from English to gibberish and back again as commanded by a partner, while you are giving a lecture or demonstration on a familiar topic. There must be no hesitation as you switch languages, if you are really transmitting ideas on both levels.

f   Build a scene in which a TV interviewer asks questions of a foreign specialist, politician, or celebrity, who speaks only gibberish and must depend on a translator to interpret the questions and his replies. Switch roles among the three of you so that all have a chance to experience each other's problems in the situation. Actual news broadcasts will provide ideas.

g   Build a scene in which primitive people are praying in a gibberish chant to one of their gods. Each native has his own reason for praying, or else all can be participating in a tribal ritual for a common goal. Assume appropriate postures (such as full length, face down, stretched toward the "god" or on knees in a keening movement). At a signal the "god" answers, and the chanting varies accordingly.

h   Build a scene at a national border customs desk, where the inspector speaks English but each tourist in the checking line speaks a different gibberish. Or have the inspector speaking gibberish to English-speaking tourists. Some high comedy—or tragedy—may result if *all* speak gibberish.

i   Try a variation on the Sound-Track exercises (Group-Ups No. 2) by presenting a love scene from a foreign film, in which the actors speak gibberish while "dubbed voices" simultaneously present English subtitles. This exercise should be for advanced sessions, as it will truly tax your concentration, imagination, and observation if it is to be well done and not played for simple farce.

SECTION SIX

DRESS-UPS

These exercises encourage you to apply what you learned in handling various objects, responding with the senses of sight and touch. Now you can add the dimension of ensemble emotional responses as you identify a character symbolized by an item of clothing. Collect a wide assortment of wearing apparel in a large box, or a movable clothing rack: all the way from period costumes to modern pieces and including single items such as coats, jackets, shirts, skirts, and shoes. In the exercises you will work with only one item at a time rather than attempt to assemble a complete outfit. If your group wishes to elaborate on Dress-Ups, you may add such accessory costume props as gloves, hats, fans, canes, holstered guns, and swords. Experimentation will help you decide which items are most useful in achieving the purpose of these exercises: to stimulate ensemble imagination and concentration in rapid changes.

1 **Group-Garments**

   a   After selecting an article of clothing from a rack, put it on, then take it off and hand it to another person, who must wear it in a different way to change its function. He then hands it to another, who changes its use anew by wearing it quite differently. The whole group participates.

   b   Everyone selects an item of clothing from the rack. Put yours on and wear it as the character it suggests to you. After a moment of adjustment to the role, mingle with the other characters: introduce yourself, reveal your attitudes and reactions to each one, and finally replace the item on the rack. Then select a new item, and repeat the exercise, transforming yourself completely. Imagination will be stressed, as well as concentration.

2 **Clothes-Call**

   a   After choosing an assortment of clothing, or being handed several odd pieces to assemble, work with a partner or two to build a scene involving the characters your several costumes suggest. Present the scene to the whole group for comment. Some very interesting situations can develop from this exercise, often profoundly moving or extremely funny.

b A difficult exercise involving clothing starts with each one of a group of three or four donning a single item representing a specific type of person. As the group converses in a circle, a signal is given, whereupon everyone removes his article and hands it to the person on his right, who puts it on and immediately becomes the suggested character. The conversation continues with the newly created characters, who must continue to speak in the manner suitable to their roles, until the signal directs another exchange of garments and characters. Concentration is developed through intense listening and observing of each one in the group; the exchange of clothing is merely a stimulus to this end.

c For advanced sessions, excerpts from Genet's plays involving symbolic costuming and masks (*The Balcony, The Maids, The Blacks*) may be paraphrased or memorized for presentation.

SECTION SEVEN

CHANGE-UPS

The important benefit from this set of exercises will come from your discussion of their values and results. Sometimes it is only by talking about our emotional responses that we can understand them well enough to recreate them for acting purposes. Expression or repression of emotion in the theatre is always a group experience between audience and actors, even when only one character is present. You know that everything in the theatre is done for an audience, to entertain or enlighten or inspire them, so the handling of emotion onstage must be disciplined through the artistic principles of good theatre. These exercises will help you to discover how your own emotional pattern can be controlled for truth in acting. Because this work introduces the most difficult step so far, it is best to start with solo exercises and gradually build to ensemble scenes.

1 **Personal Feelings** Discuss moods and feelings, their origin (people, situations, ideas), how they are expressed and repressed, and why. Distinguish between emotions and attitudes.

   a Discuss laughter as a means of expressing a variety of emotions. Experiment with types of laughter motivated by different feelings, analyzing the sensations and muscular factors, and then work with a partner to test for recognizable traits.

   b Discuss anger: its ways of expression, and how these are achieved physically; then alternate with your partner in recreating and identifying specific expressions of anger motivated by a variety of causes.

   c Other emotions or sentiments can be handled in the same way: fear, annoyance, love, affection, reverence, and so forth.

2 **Mixed Emotions** Discuss opposing types of emotions which might occur simultaneously. Analyze again the muscular factors involved, and the specific parts of your body used to convey mixed emotions.

   a Silently imagine your most prized possession, then react to its sudden loss.

   b Tell your partner about your feelings at its loss, in detail; your partner meanwhile tries to impress you with his own feelings about *his* loss.

c   Repeat this exercise, but now use as few words as possible, to intensify your feelings through such emotional symbols as facial expressions and gestures rather than words. Sometimes the mere lifting of an eyebrow or the crooking of a finger can convey much information—we seldom employ extravagant movement or expressions in public when we feel shame, embarrassment, disappointment, or regret. Indeed, the poised person usually attempts to conceal such negative reactions by assuming a studied appearance of control, which is seen in certain bodily tensions, or with the eyes either averted or intensely focused. In this exercise, confine your utterances to key words or vocal sounds only, with partial phrases conveying whole ideas, as in "broken English."

d   You have just received something highly desired, but your close friend appears and belittles it with insults. What happens as you mix your emotions?

e   Try the same exercise with two small groups, where one group has received a high honor, and then the second group appears and shows indifference, or scorn. Test yourself for the true ensemble attitude, then switch roles and repeat. After both groups have taken both roles, discuss your emotional experiences.

3 Group Moods Again, discuss opposing emotions, both subtle and involved types, as they might occur in group conflicts.

a   Build a scene wherein a group is engaged in a common activity and is interrupted by an outsider for some logical reason (a party and the landlord, tenants and a fireman, ship passengers and the captain, plane passengers and a hijacker, dinner guests and a drunk). After suitable reactions, analyze the results.

b   Get a small-group scene going and then react to an unexpected development: the ceiling begins to move down, a telegram arrives, you start to lose part of your clothing, the temperature suddenly drops or rises, furniture movers appear and take everything away, the setting suddenly changes to an extremely different locale such as another planet, a desert island, an anthill.

c   Establish a group mood out of a common activity, then experience a sudden change of mood because of an unexpected interruption from a non-human source: explorers and a cave-in, picnickers and a storm, passengers and a crash or sinking, fallout shelter victims and a mechanical failure.

d   Observe what happens during a group scene when the lights are suddenly changed, or when music begins to play and to dominate the mood. Discuss the influence of environment on mood; then repeat the scene without the actual change. Can you recreate your altered mood without the aid of the external influence? Be honest in each emotion, and you won't be dependent on clichés and stereotypes. Involvement through imagination and concentration will produce more originality than repetition. This exercise can be expanded with your own variations to induce specific mood changes, or, by having the music and/or lighting form a pattern of changes, to stimulate your memory of past situations.

e After two groups have built themselves into independent scenes, see what happens when they are brought together to carry on in one integrated situation. You will certainly have to concentrate and observe intently.

f Two groups are in opposition: strikers versus managers, patriots versus traitors, prisoners versus guards, students versus administration, parents versus children.

g Two groups are uniting: former enemies face a common foe, former religious opponents address a common problem, youth join elders in common cause, feuding families are united by a marriage. Play it for truth!

h A very stimulating and imaginative exercise, with any number of variations, is to be a member of a group which is standing casually in silence until a second group, sitting apart, starts to chant a single word over and over: "jealous," "gossip," "shame," "horror." The listening group responds spontaneously to the chant, which crescendoes to an overwhelming intensity, or diminishes till barely audible, but persists in its torturing. The two groups, listeners and chanters, can then switch roles. *Variations:* choose a word that consoles, or amuses, or worries, rather than tortures the listeners. Sometimes the chant can be in unison to a definite rhythm, or it can be spoken in individual patterns.

4 Dilemmas The characters in these suggested situations (be sure to add your own ideas) have two or more possible solutions to a conflict. They must narrow their choice to only one. Here is experience in conveying mixed emotions under tension, and justification for making the inevitable solution.

a Build a small-group scene in which several people wake up to find themselves in a strange place, unable to recall how they got there. *Dilemma:* to adjust, or to escape?

b Create situations in which people from one period of history are suddenly transported into another period. *Dilemma:* adjust, escape, exploit the situation for personal advantage, or commit suicide?

c Build a small-group scene in which one or more characters have an overdeveloped sense of taste, or smell, or imagination, or combination of these. *Dilemma:* adjust, or operate, or exploit the feature?

d Build a scene in which all the characters except one are deaf, or mute, or blind, or otherwise handicapped. *Dilemma:* Accept the odd one as leader, or slave; master, or outcast?

e   Build a scene in which everyone is very small, or very tall, or very heavy, or lighter than air, and a so-called "normal" person enters their midst. *Dilemma*: same possibilities as in *c*.

f   Build a scene around an eccentric person who is always imagining that there are people in the room or that the situation is quite different from what it really is. *Dilemma*: Companions are annoyed, or sympathetic, or cruel, or indifferent?

g   Create a situation in which the language has been lost, and several alternatives are desperately attempted. *Dilemma*: attempt to find the old one, invent a new one, or decide on non-communication?

h   Have several small groups working simultaneously to depict a world in which everything is opposite from what we expect in our world. *Example*: punishment rather than treatment for illness, but hospitalization for every criminal; nudism is the style, clothing is indecent; animals have more power than people.

i   Have a small group of twenty-first-century archeologists discover a sealed container full of objects from our time. *Dilemma*: accept these items as trash, or as treasure, or as curios for exhibition?

j   Build a dilemma-drama in which an election committee announces victory to their candidate, who they have just learned is an ex-convict. (The more recent and serious the crime, the more difficult is the dilemma; also mature persons would react to this situation much differently from adolescents.)

k   Build a dilemma-drama in which a group of people (a firm, a family) has just discovered the scandalous truth about one of them, who holds a position of high trust.

l   Build a dilemma-drama about a family that comes to a funeral parlor to view the body of a loved one returned from battle, only to find the wrong body (perhaps a different race) in the casket.

5 Transformations   This exercise has become a popular one with audiences at such improvisational shows as "Theatre Games," produced in New York and Los Angeles, in which, with suggestions from the audience, the actors mounted a number of improvised dramatic sketches composed of lightning transformations of time, place, and identity, no script and no props, and a moment-by-moment resolution. Transformations dependent on audience suggestions for setting, characters, and situation may not always be as successful in public shows as they are in the privacy of the studio. Experiment with this old-new actor's device for turning on total concentration, imagination, and observation in a dramatic ensemble.

a   Start a scene with one person who establishes the mood and locale: as a new person enters, he presents a fresh mood and locale, and both sustain the change till the next arrival brings another change, and so on till the whole group has entered in turn.

Variations on this exercise can determine whether each character shall remain the same throughout, despite the scene and mood changes, or whether the characters must also change with each new arrival.

b In partners, start as two definite characters in a situation. One observes a gesture or pose or remark made by the other, which cues a complete transformation of setting and characters. The trick here is the complete and immediate change, without the slightest hesitation on either part. Changes should occur as frequently as possible, allowing only enough time to establish the new situation and roles. Neither of the partners has any way of knowing which of them will make the next change, nor what it will be. Total concentration, imagination, and observation are involved in this exercise. It can be quite exhausting but fun, especially if clichés are avoided, and truth is conveyed at each turn.

c *Variations*: End the series of transformations exactly as it started, with characters and setting the same. Or, for a further challenge, with the characters switched!

Ask Yourself

After a number of sessions have included exercises from each of the units in Part Two (Group-Ups, Dress-Ups, Change-Ups), test your progress with these questions and others that may have occurred to you. Space is allowed for written answers, in case you wish to submit them to your instructor for further advice on your Ensemble Attitude.

1 Can I coordinate my actions and speech with a partner so well that we can usually anticipate each other's ideas prior to their expression?

2 Can I concentrate on two or more partners in a scene at the same time that I am projecting my own character?

3 Can I share a scene with others by doing and saying things which help to develop their characters as well as my own?

4 Can I underplay at times to help the focus shift to others within a scene rather than keeping it on myself or my group by excessive speech or action?

5 Am I able to make believable physical contact with others in a scene without self-consciousness or inhibition?

6 Can I carry on conversation while employed in complex physical activity?

7 Can I carry on conversation while handling objects in a complicated pattern?

8 Do I experience a true feeling of unity with others when engaged in a group scene of simple or silent action?

9 Am I able to concentrate on character and purpose despite continuous interruptions or distractions from others in the scene?

10 Am I able to help build a scene of intense emotion without resorting to verbal or physical extremity?

11 Can I communicate with one other person or several others in a scene by vocal means besides recognizable language?

12 Is my concentration sufficient to convey ideas in a logical line of thought despite sudden changes from English to gibberish?

13 Can I help build a scene for intentional comic application of techniques without always resorting to slapstick or farce?

14 Can I help build a scene for intentional dramatic application of techniques without always resorting to melodrama or trajedy?

15 Am I able to recognize and respond to character changes in others by merely a quick observation of such unspoken behavior as the use of a costume piece or prop?

16 Can I distinguish between emotions and attitudes?

17 Can I explain the origin, expression, and repression of moods and feelings as part of human interaction?

18 Can I experience and convincingly express two contrasting emotions simultaneously?

19 In an intense conversational scene, can I convey extreme emotion with very few words?

20 Can I listen intently and understandingly to others in a scene, even though my own character is under a strain?

21 Am I able to experience a controversy from both sides by switching roles yet retaining sincere involvement with either character?

22 Am I able to adjust quickly to situation changes and still continue developing my character in relation to the others in the scene?

23 Can I contribute to the development of a logical resolution despite what effect it may have on my character, or on my personal preference of a solution?

24 Do I always strive to seek the truth about my character and express it convincingly in relation to plot complexities and the other characters in the scene?

25 Do I always attempt to achieve a base of believability through my character, regardless of fantastic situations or fanciful characters in the scene?

26 Do I dedicate myself to the group effort at creating a believable scene, whether the style be comic or serious?

27 Do I allow each situation and group of characters to stimulate my imagination so that I can develop an original character and business, and avoid clichés and stereotypes?

28 (Write in special questions from your instructor) _____

_____

_____

_____

(If you hand in your answers, fill in below.)

Signed _____

Date _____

Ask Your Instructor

As in Part One, use these questions to stimulate group discussion, or as a hand-in assignment.

1 Are we successfully applying the principles of improvisation we learned in the Daily Exercises?

2 Do we understand what an ensemble involves, in contrast to solo exercises?

3 Are we able to integrate our individual efforts into a cohesive group activity?

4 Do we show any preference for a particular style of playing? (Farce, high comedy, melodrama, social drama, fantasy.)

5 Do we listen and observe so that our action develops from reaction?

6 Is our sense of ensemble timing improving?

7 Is our sense of ensemble tempo improving?

8 Do we avoid a "star" or a "playwright" type of ensemble leadership?

9 Are we ready for full Characterization Exercises?

Part Three

Characterization Exercises

Now we have arrived at the point where principles learned from all the exercises are applied. We have been following a gradual development of your body and emotions and imagination, sometimes with speech and props, sometimes without, which has led us to the main problem of the actor: to present a living person other than himself. The following exercises in characterization will help you to discipline what you have learned so far, and to create a person in terms of the truth about that person, not in terms of yourself. The only restriction you will have in this process is to stay with your own sex and stature, keeping in mind the possibility that you could publicly portray the character you create through these exercises.

Sometimes a character cannot be developed beyond a certain point: he may have unexpected limitations, an enclosed personality. In that case, you must reject him and select another more "stage-worthy." Sometimes a character will move into an entirely new dimension, requiring a careful evaluation of the extent to which he has developed after a number of situations have tested him for consistent truth.

Each exercise is a new situation, so that you will not be able to preplan or write out a scene. Your character must establish relationships with all the other created characters and not depend on the same one or two for developing each scene. In other words, "playwriting" must be avoided if spontaneity is to work.

SECTION EIGHT

ACT-UPS

Again, we start with simple situations and work into more complex ones, discovering the truths necessary to convey the ideas. But now, for each exercise there will be some paper work for the purpose of preparation and grading. Before presenting a character, fill out and hand in the worksheets at the end of this section. Each time you present the character in the following exercises, hand a properly headed Grading Guide to the instructor. Save the worksheets and grading guides (pp. 71-89) as a set of basic steps to aid in your characterization process for roles you may wish to play in the future.

Now, to the exercises for characterization development:

1 Imitations As in Parts One and Two stimulate your C.I.O. faculties to get started.

a Imitate yourself engaged in a very familiar daily occupation; then repeat the action under an emotional stress by inventing a vital reason for doing it—a purpose that arouses some sort of emotion in you. Present this emotional version, without speech, to the whole group. Do you communicate the situation? Do they understand *why* you are doing that particular task? Do they recognize the emotion?

Example: Indifferently shine your shoes. Then shine them for a job interview, or the first date with a new friend, for your wedding, or the funeral of a loved one.

Example: Indifferently wash the dishes. Then wash them before important company arrives, or after a wild party, for the first time after buying them, or for the last time before giving them to your children.

b Imitate someone you know whom you can study for total detail. Engage that person in a familiar daily occupation, and present him or her (choose one of your sex and age) without speech to the whole group. Let them describe the person to you on the basis of what they see. Note that this is not impersonation or interpretation, but duplication! Be honest and fair.

c Work further on your Imitation Character by adding voice, and by building more complex situations, even imaginary ones which that person would hardly be expected to experience. Test yourself for accuracy and consistency as you apply concentration, imagination, and observation.

d   Now you are ready to use one of the blank worksheets for a Six-Segment Character Analysis (pp. 71-79). Evaluate your imitation Character for these six factors: (*1*) age, (*2*) physical presence, (*3*) clothing and accessories, (*4*) temperament, (*5*) experience (background), (*6*) general attitude and outlook on life. Give the completed worksheet to your instructor for his reaction and comment.

e   Present your Imitation Character in a series of scenes in which each of the six factors is featured in order to familiarize yourself with him as thoroughly as possible.

Example: A scene in which your Imitation Character's physical presence is demonstrated might include action of weighing himself at home, or seeing himself in distorted mirrors at the carnival fun house, or trying on outgrown clothing from an old trunk.

Example: The background experience of your Imitation Character might be revealed when he replies to interview questions for a job or insurance, when he talks about himself as part of a marriage proposal, or when he defends his reputation in a court case.

2 Creating a Character   Now that you have acquainted yourself with the Six-Segment Character Analysis worksheet through your Imitation Character, you can proceed to create a wholly original person.

a   Use a blank worksheet to analyze yourself in terms of the six basic segments of a stage character. Be objective about yourself— this may not be easy! Do not hand this in, as it is a private aid to an honest self-evaluation.

b   Imagine a person who is extremely different from yourself in each of the six basic segments. Note that some differences may be more desirable than others. You might be tempted to create a horrid character in self-defense, but the purpose here is to choose not *opposite* features, just "extremely different" ones.

Example: Supposing your own clothing and accessories reflect a rather flamboyant personality—bright colors, bold patterns, flaring and flowing garments, no stockings, leather sandals, and long, loose hair. Your Created Character then could be much more conservative, choosing dull colors and patterns, tight-fitting clothes, perhaps high boots or heavy shoes and stockings, and close-cropped hair. Remember that clothing and accessories should be depended upon not for building your character but for depicting a part of his personality that has been determined by the other factors. An actor does not believe that "clothes make the man," but he does understand that appearance is a stimulating commentary on a person's values and habits. That is why we do not wait until dress rehearsal to "get into character"; the process of creating a character does not separate the outer from the inner man, whether onstage or in life.

Example: Supposing your own outlook on life is pessimistic; you are unable to see any solutions to world or local problems, with even a trace of despair underlying your preference for theatre as an escape from reality. Then your Created Character might be generally optimistic, but a realist in facing problems, with even a slight contempt for theatrical people.

c   When you have created this person in your mind, on a blank worksheet write a complete analysis of him, including each of the six segments, in the style of an autobiography. That is, let him speak for himself on each point, although you may have to insert an "editor's comment" of your own if he is not always honest. If your Created Character is unable to write, you must fill out the worksheet for him as if from dictation. Submit your Created Character's autobiography for evaluation and correction. Revise it on additional worksheets as needed. If your character is the type who keeps a diary, be sure you make *daily* entries for him as long as he "lives."

d   The Grading Guide sheets on pp. 81-89 may be requested by your instructor each time your Created Character is presented in any of the exercises following in No. 3, "Peeling the Orange." Study this Grading Guide as a reminder of what you are expected to convey through your Created Character.

3 Peeling the Orange   Now you are going to uncover each of the six basic factors comprising the personality of your Created Character. In effect, it is like peeling away the rind that encloses the six-segment "heart" of an orange. And because it is spherical, it is a unified whole; that is, each segment fits with each other segment just as each factor in your character's makeup is interdependent with every other factor. Understanding this principle in characterization will prevent you from resorting to stereotypes or cliché mannerisms.

a   Your Created Character must be interviewed by someone (instructor? director? guest?) following the Six-Segment Character Analysis you have submitted, encouraging you through penetrating questions to enlarge on what you have written. This is a revealing experience about the consistency and honesty of the character, as well as your own attention to detail.

Example: If your Created Character walks with a slight limp and has dark brown complexion, his temperament may tend toward impatience or resignation, determined by when and how he acquired the limp, by his financial and educational status, and by his philosophy. Consequently, he chooses clothing and accessories that reflect these factors of his personality.

Example: If your Created Character has always been a physically beautiful person, receiving constant praise and prizes, the temperament may be either extremely vain or humble, according to influences in childhood training, experiences in human relations, economic status, and so forth. Naturally, clothing and accessories will seem important to this person, but what kind of outlook on life will have developed?

b Now that your "Orange Character" has been presented to the group through the interview situation, place him in a series of daily routines, simple occupations, and observe him for truth in every detail. Don't overlook hands, feet, and subtle mannerisms. Is your Orange Friend ever imitating *you*? And is he becoming truly a *friend*? You will learn quickly whether or not you are in the truth of the character as you have created him. Accept all ideas that come to you—don't block any action, unless the truth of the character is involved. Discuss your discoveries before proceeding. If, after these everyday situations and the interview, you find that you cannot possibly accept this person, you will have to drop him and start over again.

c *Think* as the character would during certain moments of your own daily routine. How does the character drive your car, enter or leave your house, eat at your table? (It may be best if you let him take over only when there are no observers who might be confused by your unfamiliar behavior.)

d Choose a classmate whose Created Character could develop a scene with yours. Establish a logical relationship in a real-life situation, but stress believable human elements more than plot or setting.

Example: Supposing the two Created Characters in examples for 3-*a* (the interview) get together for a scene. Dark-Brown Limp and Beautiful Person may find much in common, or even a sympathetic attraction, depending on their temperaments and outlooks. Where might they meet? Would Dark-Brown Limp be a judge at a contest in which Beautiful Person is a winner? Or a talent agent-and-client relationship? Or a teacher-student, husband-wife, parent-child relationship? With imagination and observation you can develop infinite variations on most any combination.

e Ensemble scenes may be difficult at first, until you find some common ground for all the Created Characters to assemble. Waiting rooms (doctor, dentist, lawyer, hotel, terminal) are possibilities. Perhaps one character could be landlord to the rest, all residents in the same apartment building. You might all be passengers (plane, train, ship, tour bus) or patients in a hospital ward, or disaster victims in a shelter (flood, fire, or fallout). Group efforts in imagination will be necessary.

f Out of the ensemble scenes may arise a genuine relationship among several of the characters. You might join in presenting a spontaneous scene of your own, just to see how far you can realize the truth of your reactions.

g When the Created Characters have appeared in enough scenes to determine whether the six-segment orange has been successfully "peeled," your group may decide to "eliminate" these characters. This may be accomplished in one ensemble scene wherein a fatal action occurs, on or off stage, to each character in his turn. Possible settings could be the waiting room of a concentration camp (each character will have to justify clearly how he happens to be there, regardless of the national politics involved), and an offstage voice calls each one to his execution; or all are on a plane or ocean liner, as passengers or employees, and there is a crash or sinking that allows each one to demonstrate his final action in the ordeal; or they could all be in a fallout shelter under nuclear attack, and as the oxygen gives out each one reveals his own way of meeting his end. Let your imagination, as well as your observation of current events, lead you to develop a logical situation for your character to meet the demise that is true for him: honorable, inspired, ignoble, selfish, hysterical, horrible, and so forth.

4 Discussing Characterizations After the Created Characters have been "eliminated," participate in a series of reports and discussions on the techniques involved in creating them. As a result, you may find it easier to develop your own technique of characterization, which will inevitably lead to your own special acting style, marking you as an individual interpreter, but hopefully not as either a one-dimensional "personality" performer or a fanatic for a single theory of acting.

a Discuss how you built your Created Character, and the means you discovered for staying in character despite the situations or conflicting relationships.

b At this point your instructor may feel it would be helpful to consult what famous actors have said (in print or recordings) about their techniques of characterization. Use the form titled "Report: Techniques of Characterization" (pp. 91-99) to submit your total findings on a favorite performer's technique, or on the same technique used by a number of performers.

c If you report on a performer, be sure to include his age, nationality, the medium in which he is best known (film, stage, TV), some details about his training and experience, and some direct quotations on his theory of acting.

d If you report about one technique used by several performers, explain that technique in detail, then identify those who use it and their ideas about it.

Worksheet: Six-Segment Character Analysis

"Reporter" _____

Date _____

Grade _____

Check one:

_____ Imitation Character (Act-Ups 1-*d*)

_____ Self-analysis   (Act-Ups 2-*a*)

_____ Created Character   (Act-Ups 2-*c*)

Subject's name _____ *Nickname(s)* _____

Please answer the following autobiographical questionnaire as briefly and accurately as possible. Where needed for clarification, editorial comments may be added by the "reporter" on an additional worksheet.

1   Birthdate _____ Present age _____

2   Height _____ Weight _____ Diet? _____

    Color hair _____ Color eyes _____ Complexion _____

    Deformities? _____ Handicaps? _____

    Diseases? _____ General health _____

3   My usual style of clothing _____

    _____

    My usual types of accessories _____

    _____

4   My temperament could be described as _____

    For example _____

    _____

5   My background includes a childhood influenced by (family? friends? education? religion? socioeconomic advantages or disadvantages?) _____

    _____

    Certain experiences or occupations have made lasting impressions _____

    _____

    _____

6 My general attitude and outlook on life have been determined by _____

_____

_____

Above all else, I sincerely believe _____

_____

_____

Worksheet: Six-Segment Character Analysis

"Reporter" _____

Date _____

Grade _____

Check one:

_____ Imitation Character (Act-Ups 1-*d*)

_____ Self-analysis   (Act-Ups 2-*a*)

_____ Created Character   (Act-Ups 2-*c*)

Subject's name _____ *Nickname(s)* _____

Please answer the following autobiographical questionnaire as briefly and accurately as possible. Where needed for clarification, editorial comments may be added by the "reporter" on an additional worksheet.

1 Birthdate _____ Present age _____

2 Height _____ Weight _____ Diet? _____

   Color hair _____ Color eyes _____ Complexion _____

   Deformities? _____ Handicaps? _____

   Diseases? _____ General health _____

3 My usual style of clothing _____

   _____

   My usual types of accessories _____

   _____

4 My temperament could be described as _____

   For example _____

   _____

5 My background includes a childhood influenced by (family? friends? education? religion? socioeconomic advantages or disadvantages?) _____

   _____

   Certain experiences or occupations have made lasting impressions _____

   _____

   _____

6 My general attitude and outlook on life have been determined by _____

_____

_____

Above all else, I sincerely believe _____

_____

_____

Worksheet: Six-Segment Character Analysis

"Reporter" _____

Date _____

Grade _____

Check one:

_____ Imitation Character (Act-Ups 1-*d*)

_____ Self-analysis   (Act-Ups 2-*a*)

_____ Created Character   (Act-Ups 2-*c*)

Subject's name _____ *Nickname(s)* _____

Please answer the following autobiographical questionnaire as briefly and accurately as possible. Where needed for clarification, editorial comments may be added by the "reporter" on an additional worksheet.

1 Birthdate _____ Present age _____

2 Height _____ Weight _____ Diet? _____

   Color hair _____ Color eyes _____ Complexion _____

   Deformities? _____ Handicaps? _____

   Diseases? _____ General health _____

3 My usual style of clothing _____

   _____

   My usual types of accessories _____

   _____

4 My temperament could be described as _____

   For example _____

5 My background includes a childhood influenced by (family? friends? education? religion? socioeconomic advantages or disadvantages?) _____

   _____

   Certain experiences or occupations have made lasting impressions _____

   _____

   _____

6 My general attitude and outlook on life have been determined by _____

_____

_____

Above all else, I sincerely believe _____

_____

_____

Worksheet: Six-Segment Character Analysis

"Reporter" _____

Date _____

Grade _____

Check one:

_____ Imitation Character (Act-Ups 1-*d*)

_____ Self-analysis   (Act-Ups 2-*a*)

_____ Created Character   (Act-Ups 2-*c*)

Subject's name _____ *Nickname(s)* _____

Please answer the following autobiographical questionnaire as briefly and accurately as possible. Where needed for clarification, editorial comments may be added by the "reporter" on an additional worksheet.

1 Birthdate _____ Present age _____

2 Height _____ Weight _____ Diet? _____

   Color hair _____ Color eyes _____ Complexion _____

   Deformities? _____ Handicaps? _____

   Diseases? _____ General health _____

3 My usual style of clothing _____

   _____

   My usual types of accessories _____

   _____

4 My temperament could be described as _____

   For example _____

   _____

5 My background includes a childhood influenced by (family? friends? education? religion? socioeconomic advantages or disadvantages?) _____

   _____

   Certain experiences or occupations have made lasting impressions _____

   _____

   _____

6 My general attitude and outlook on life have been determined by _____

_____

_____

Above all else, I sincerely believe _____

_____

_____

Worksheet: Six-Segment Character Analysis

"Reporter" _____

⌐Date _____

Grade _____

Check one:

_____ Imitation Character (Act-Ups 1-*d*)

_____ Self-analysis   (Act-Ups 2-*a*)

_____ Created Character   (Act-Ups 2-*c*)

Subject's name _____ *Nickname(s)* _____

Please answer the following autobiographical questionnaire as briefly and accurately as possible. Where needed for clarification, editorial comments may be added by the "reporter" on an additional worksheet.

1 Birthdate _____ Present age _____

2 Height _____ Weight _____ Diet? _____

Color hair _____ Color eyes _____ Complexion _____

Deformities? _____ Handicaps? _____

Diseases? _____ General health _____

3 My usual style of clothing _____

_____

My usual types of accessories _____

_____

4 My temperament could be described as _____

For example _____

_____

5 My background includes a childhood influenced by (family? friends? education? religion? socioeconomic advantages or disadvantages?) _____

_____

Certain experiences or occupations have made lasting impressions _____

_____

_____

6 My general attitude and outlook on life have been determined by _____

_____

_____

Above all else, I sincerely believe _____

_____

_____

Grading Guide

Character _____   Name _____

Situation _____   Date _____

_____   Grade _____

Key: 0 = Absent or unprepared   3 = Effective, believable

      1 = Weak, needs much work   4 = Excellent, professional quality

      2 = Satisfactory, but try harder

Score	*Specific Factor*	*Comments*
( )	Age	1
( )	Physical appearance	2
( )	Clothing, Accessories	3
( )	Temperament	4
( )	Background, Experience	5
( )	Attitude, Outlook	6

General Technique

( )	Concentration	7
( )	Imagination	8
( )	Observation	9
( )	Movement	10
( )	Voice and diction	11
( )	Ensemble	12
( )	_____	13
( )	_____	14
( )	_____	15
( )	*Total*	
( )	*Possible Score:* 4 × Number graded	

(Note: 13, 14, and 15 will be added by instructor for special areas in current study.)

Grading Guide

Character _____ Name _____

Situation _____ Date _____

_____ Grade _____

Key: 0 = Absent or unprepared   3 = Effective, believable
      1 = Weak, needs much work   4 = Excellent, professional quality
      2 = Satisfactory, but try harder

Score	Specific Factor	Comments
( )	Age	1
( )	Physical appearance	2
( )	Clothing, Accessories	3
( )	Temperament	4
( )	Background, Experience	5
( )	Attitude, Outlook	6

General Technique

( )	Concentration	7
( )	Imagination	8
( )	Observation	9
( )	Movement	10
( )	Voice and diction	11
( )	Ensemble	12
( )	_____	13
( )	_____	14
( )	_____	15

( ) *Total*

( ) *Possible Score:* 4 X Number graded

(Note: 13, 14, and 15 will be added by instructor for special areas in current study.)

Grading Guide

Character _____ Name _____

Situation _____ Date _____

_____ Grade _____

Key: 0 = Absent or unprepared   3 = Effective, believable

1 = Weak, needs much work   4 = Excellent, professional quality

2 = Satisfactory, but try harder

Score	Specific Factor	Comments
( )	Age	1
( )	Physical appearance	2
( )	Clothing, Accessories	3
( )	Temperament	4
( )	Background, Experience	5
( )	Attitude, Outlook	6

General Technique

( )	Concentration	7
( )	Imagination	8
( )	Observation	9
( )	Movement	10
( )	Voice and diction	11
( )	Ensemble	12
( )	_____	13
( )	_____	14
( )	_____	15
( )	*Total*	
( )	*Possible Score:* 4 X Number graded	

(Note: 13, 14, and 15 will be added by instructor for special areas in current study.)

Grading Guide

Character _____ Name _____

Situation _____ Date _____

_____ Grade _____

Key: 0 = Absent or unprepared   3 = Effective, believable

1 = Weak, needs much work   4 = Excellent, professional quality

2 = Satisfactory, but try harder

Score	Specific Factor	Comments
( )	Age	1
( )	Physical appearance	2
( )	Clothing, Accessories	3
( )	Temperament	4
( )	Background, Experience	5
( )	Attitude, Outlook	6
	General Technique	
( )	Concentration	7
( )	Imagination	8
( )	Observation	9
( )	Movement	10
( )	Voice and diction	11
( )	Ensemble	12
( )	_____	13
( )	_____	14
( )	_____	15
( )	*Total*	
( )	*Possible Score:* 4 X Number graded	

(Note: 13, 14, and 15 will be added by instructor for special areas in current study.)

Grading Guide

Character _____   Name _____

Situation _____   Date _____

_____   Grade _____

Key: 0 = Absent or unprepared   3 = Effective, believable
         1 = Weak, needs much work   4 = Excellent, professional quality
         2 = Satisfactory, but try harder

Score	*Specific Factor*	*Comments*
( )	Age	1
( )	Physical appearance	2
( )	Clothing, Accessories	3
( )	Temperament	4
( )	Background, Experience	5
( )	Attitude, Outlook	6

General Technique

( )	Concentration	7
( )	Imagination	8
( )	Observation	9
( )	Movement	10
( )	Voice and diction	11
( )	Ensemble	12
( )	_____	13
( )	_____	14
( )	_____	15
( )	*Total*	
( )	*Possible Score:* 4 × Number graded	

(Note: 13, 14, and 15 will be added by instructor for special areas in current study.)

Report: Techniques of Characterization

Submitted by _____

Date _____

Grade _____

(based on accuracy, depth, clarity of
presentation in oral or written form)

Source 1 _____

Source 2 _____

Source 3 _____

_____

_____

Actor or Actress: _____

or

Specific Acting Technique: _____

(Consider for either type of report the national and artistic traditions which may have subtle or obvious influences on your subject. Consult the Bibliography at the end of this book for a few good references to start on.)

Report: Techniques of Characterization

Submitted by _____

Date _____

Grade _____

(based on accuracy, depth, clarity of
presentation in oral or written form)

Source 1 _____

Source 2 _____

Source 3 _____

_____

_____

Actor or Actress:_____

or

Specific Acting Technique: _____

(Consider for either type of report the national and artistic traditions which may have subtle or
obvious influences on your subject. Consult the Bibliography at the end of this book for a few
good references to start on.)

Report: Techniques of Characterization

Submitted by _____

Date _____

Grade _____

(based on accuracy, depth, clarity of
presentation in oral or written form)

Source 1 _____

Source 2 _____

Source 3 _____

_____

_____

Actor or Actress: _____

or

Specific Acting Technique: _____

(Consider for either type of report the national and artistic traditions which may have subtle or
obvious influences on your subject. Consult the Bibliography at the end of this book for a few
good references to start on.)

Report: Techniques of Characterization

Submitted by _____

Date _____

Grade _____

(based on accuracy, depth, clarity of
presentation in oral or written form)

Source 1 _____

Source 2 _____

Source 3 _____

_____

_____

Actor or Actress: _____

or

Specific Acting Technique: _____

(Consider for either type of report the national and artistic traditions which may have subtle or
obvious influences on your subject. Consult the Bibliography at the end of this book for a few
good references to start on.)

Report: Techniques of Characterization

Submitted by _____

Date _____

Grade _____
(based on accuracy, depth, clarity of
presentation in oral or written form)

Source 1 _____

Source 2 _____

Source 3 _____

_____

_____

Actor or Actress:_____

or

Specific Acting Technique: _____

(Consider for either type of report the national and artistic traditions which may have subtle or
obvious influences on your subject. Consult the Bibliography at the end of this book for a few
good references to start on.)

SECTION NINE

SHAPE-UPS

Now you are ready to focus on performance problems from the audience's point of view. Until now *you* have been the central person in each scene, but perhaps you have not always grasped the purpose behind your solo exercises and ensemble scenes. It is this: to communicate an idea to an observer.

In conventional theatre, observers sit in a designated area and watch your action or interaction with other performers. In some forms of contemporary theatre, observers sit in several areas, called "islands," watching your performance from various angles; in some extreme avant-garde theatre, observers participate in the action in varying degrees, no longer confined to chairs in clusters but surrounded by the action at all times. It is not our purpose here to evaluate the effectiveness of such productions but to point out the greater potential for movement now permitted the actor, with the new problem of projection that accompanies such freedom.

If your audience no longer sees you as a picture in a frame (proscenium or end-staging), but now surrounds you; or, even more difficult, if *you* surround the audience in your action—just how do you decide in which direction to focus your voice (always of primary importance) on key speeches, or your face and hands on "plot" business? Trust your director, and your aesthetic instinct, and your sense of timing, and your fellow-actors, and, of course, the playwright—unless you are engaged in a public program of improvisations. At this point let us remind ourselves that the improvisational exercises in this book are essentially a means to an end: the successful interpretation of a playwright's ideas; and not an end in itself: a public performance of actors' ideas.

However, in contemporary theatre, improvisations have entertained many audiences because of the spontaneity and freshness possible with imagination serving both actors and observers. But that freshness is soon lost when the actors begin incorporating successful "bits" (business or speeches of stereotyped caricatures) from previous "improvs" into every new sketch. Improvised acting is cheating, in a sense, but as a tradition it stretches from the classic Greek comedies (which enabled actors to develop spontaneous horseplay satirizing certain public figures in the audience), to the Roman "ludi" (ludicrous clownings), to the devilish pranks of Satan in the medieval church plays, to the commedia dell'arte of Renaissance Italy (professional troupes whose stock comic characters appeared in all their plays, which were improvised from mere plot outlines), to modern circus clowns and variety entertainers in night clubs and television. In each of these forms, however, when the style loses its spontaneous quality, improvisation as an end in itself ceases to amuse us and even becomes embarrassing.

Therefore, let us remind ourselves constantly that improvisation is still most effective when it is a means to that very important end: truth in acting. We perceive the acting as the interpretation of recognized dramatic literature to an audience for their entertainment, enlightenment, and often, we hope, their inspiration, and not as inbred self-indulgence, satisfying the actors themselves more than the audience and becoming a therapeutic rather than an artistic expression.

To understand more about this business of "truth in acting," let us now consider some specific disciplines in our preparatory improvisational work: structure and communication.

1 Improvisation for Structure

a   Discuss with your group the problems you have all encountered in developing ensemble scenes so far, such as:

(1) How can we prevent one or two persons from dominating a scene's development? (We call this "playwriting.")

(2) How can we shift the focus from one person or group to another so that "scene stealing" is minimized and action develops evenly among all present?

(3) How can we make better use of exposition so that the conflict is logical and dramatically sound?

(4) How can we move from the conflict so that everyone participating recognizes that point at which the resolution must begin and actually come to a logical conclusion based on the characters themselves, and not on some *deus ex machina*?

b   List examples of possibilities in structuring a scene after evaluating such aspects as:

(1) How many ways is it possible to *open a scene*? That is, should there always be at least one person on stage? Or, conversely, should action always start with a dialogue, or a monologue or soliloquy? Should the opening always occur at a moment preceding the conflict, or could it open when the conflict is just developing?

(*Example:* in the dilemma scene in which an election committee announcing victory to their candidate discovers that he is an ex-convict—would it be more dramatic to open the scene at the moment they are learning about his past, or at the moment he enters to hear their announcement, or at the moment he decides whether or not to accept the victory? Be aware that if you play it for all three moments you may have a thirty-minute one-act play to develop, which may be far from your original goal.)

(2) How many ways is it possible to *build the exposition into a conflict*? Is it inevitable to have two characters discuss past events leading to the opening action? Writers of drama have done this for centuries, hence so many maids and butlers, or gossipy neighbors, or friends of protagonists—even Shakespeare's greatest play, *Hamlet*, opens with Horatio (the Ideal Friend) discussing pre-curtain action with the palace guards. Past action is sometimes summarized in a letter just received and read aloud, and the telegram and telephone have become important devices for exposition. How often have you seen a drama in which a radio (in the home, on the beach, in the patrol car, in the airplane cockpit) is the medium for exposition—or even television providing a well-timed news bulletin? How about the "self-destruct" tape-recorded message that effectively briefed the "non-destruct" hero on the major conflict elements in the long-run TV melodrama series "Mission: Impossible"? The possibilities are as wide as your imagination.

(3) How many *types of conflicts* can be logically developed in a short scene? If the three basic conflicts are Man versus Man, Man versus Nature, and Man versus Himself, how many variations can you and your group pursue from just one of these regardless of the situation and characters? For example, consider another of the dilemma scenes: through an unknown force, a group of people has suddenly lost its spoken and written language. They react as individuals; yet they must still be an ensemble. Will they fight among themselves to establish a new communicative means? (Man versus Man) Or will they unite to search for a way out, or desperately pray together for some divine deliverance? (Man versus Nature) Or will they split totally and each work independently to overcome his deeply personal handicap of non-communication? (Man versus Himself) Of course, the type of people involved will determine the truth of the conflict: a group of scholars or artists would certainly react differently from a group of hard-hat laborers, or minority militants, or children under twelve. As you begin each scene, try to discover which of the three basic conflicts would be the core of the situation—perhaps, if your group is imaginative and observant enough, you will discover a blending of two or all three conflicts developing simultaneously.

(4) How many ways are there to *resolve a scene*? Must the ending be happy or sad every time? Can there be one in which a question is left unanswered? For example, can the ex-convict be left alone to make his decision about accepting the high public office, and the scene be ended on his dilemma? This would surely force an audience to think, and, if it has been believably acted, the audience response would be neither totally sympathetic to nor totally alienated from the central character. At such a point, the basic conflict of Man versus Himself would involve each member of the audience—which is perhaps the highest achievement of any drama.

Yet such an ending might not be effective for every scene. Some episodes can have meaning only if they have a clear-cut conclusion. George Bernard Shaw wrote two conclusions for his play *Pygmalion* so that his friends and critics could take their preference. One famous old courtroom drama, *The Night of January 16th,* is resolved by a jury made up of audience members at each performance, who give their verdict after deliberation during the final intermission, thus determining which ending the cast will enact. But with an improvised scene, the resolution must grow out of the actors themselves as they observe the logical development of the crisis and the truth of the characters involved.

(5) How should a *scene be concluded*? If there is no one to turn out the lights or to drop a curtain, should all the characters be motivated to leave the stage? Or should they all drop dead, or freeze into a tableau? What if someone doesn't want to end it there, even after the conflict has been resolved? How do you stop him from trying to carry on the scene? Should it be up to one of the spectators to call "Blackout!" or "Slow Dimout!" or "Curtain!"? How can the ensemble attain such a peak of unanimity that they collectively know that the ending has been reached? Such instinctive moments rarely happen to an acting group, but when they do, the thrill of artistic harmony is almost overwhelming. It is surely something worth striving for, because it is good theatre.

2 Improvisation for Communication What are some other difficulties your group has encountered in choosing situations or characters that present the greatest challenge? Which scenes have you done that seem least rewarding to an audience, despite the pleasure you had in doing them? Can you determine the cause of the weaknesses?

a Discuss specific problems your group has encountered in communicating ideas through words or action to an audience. Consider traditional techniques of conventional theatre, contrasted with avant-garde production techniques. In all instances, try for clarity and immediacy of communication for a desired audience response. Should they laugh, cry, be puzzled, or sigh? Review, perhaps restage, some past exercises, trying to evoke a specific and different audience response with each approach to the same material. Then evaluate what you did, how you did it, and which was the most believable style for that particular scene. Use the Grading Guide to determine your own strengths and weaknesses in each presentation. This may help to demonstrate which styles of acting you find most comfortable, and which ones you need to develop to be able to play a wider range of roles.

b Consider the total visual impression in a scene. Restage one of your favorites from the exercises, and concentrate on the use of stage areas; how the setting can be utilized for groupings, poses, tableaux, movements, entrances, and exits; when to employ such stage maneuvers as the basic Triangle Group; how to avoid "chorus lineups," about Quarter Front, Full Front, Half Right and Left, and Full Back positions, about curved and straight crosses, and timing of entrances and exits with a specific line or action.

c   Select a favorite scene from one of the exercises, or make up a new one, and stage it in four different "theatres": proscenium (end-staging), thrust (horseshoe, or three-fourths), arena (four-sided), and total (island action among dispersed audience sections).

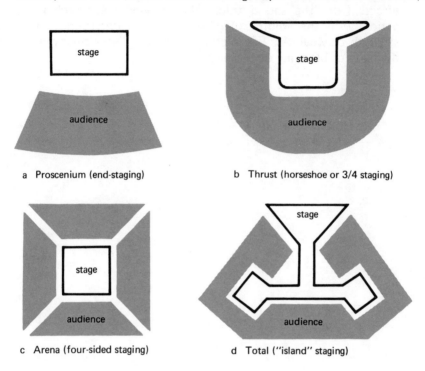

a   Proscenium (end-staging)

b   Thrust (horseshoe or 3/4 staging)

c   Arena (four-sided staging)

d   Total ("island" staging)

Four Stage Areas

Follow-up discussion will evaluate how well you adapted to audience projection each time, how your speaking and movement were regulated by the setting changes according to the audience location, and how some of the dialogue and action was also affected by the physical factors. It may be advisable for you to use the Stage Area worksheets (pp. 107-115) to illustrate the positions and movements of a given moment in either an improvised or a memorized scene, as it would be adapted to each of the four areas.

d   Experiment with one of your successful ensemble scenes, in whatever form of staging, and try to improve its visual effects as a means of communicating subtle as well as obvious ideas. For this experiment you may find it helpful to concentrate fully on the visual by subordinating dialogue to gibberish or to totally silent action, but not resorting to sign language since all participants will already know the plot and characters. Concentrate on observable factors only. How well do you handle furniture, props, the set itself? How believable are your physical contacts with others? How consistent are your gestures, poses, movements, facial expressions in conveying the six basic segments of your character?

e   If a video-tape recorder is available, use it for group criticism of one of these ensemble efforts to evaluate the visual effects of a scene. During the playback, cover the screen and listen to the aural effects from the sound track; then rewind and watch the same action with the volume off. This will help determine where the strength or weakness lies in communicating a particular moment in dialogue or blocking or business.

Worksheet: Stage Areas

Name _____

Scene _____   Date _____

Characters _____   Grade _____

Key: Character (first initial)

Chair ▽   Table □   Sofa ◡

1 PROSCENIUM (end-staging)   *Stage Directions and Comments*

2 THRUST (horseshoe, three-fourths)

3 ARENA (four-sided)

4 TOTAL (island staging)

Worksheet: Stage Areas

Name _____

Scene _____   Date _____

Characters _____   Grade _____

Key: Character (first initial)

Chair ⬡   Table ▢   Sofa ⬡

1 PROSCENIUM (end-staging)   *Stage Directions and Comments*

2 THRUST (horseshoe, three-fourths)

3 ARENA (four-sided)

4 TOTAL (island staging)

Worksheet: Stage Areas

Name _____

Scene _____   Date _____

Characters _____   Grade _____

Key: Character (first initial)

Chair ⬭   Table ☐   Sofa ⬭

1 PROSCENIUM (end-staging)	*Stage Directions and Comments*
2 THRUST (horseshoe, three-fourths)	
3 ARENA (four-sided)	
4 TOTAL (island staging)	

Worksheet: Stage Areas

Name _____

Scene _____ Date _____

Characters _____ Grade _____

Key: Character (first initial)

Chair ▽ Table ☐ Sofa ▽

1 PROSCENIUM (end-staging)	*Stage Directions and Comments*
2 THRUST (horseshoe, three-fourths)	
3 ARENA (four-sided)	
4 TOTAL (island staging)	

Worksheet: Stage Areas

Name _____

Scene _____   Date _____

Characters _____   Grade _____

Key: Character (first initial)

Chair ⌣   Table ☐   Sofa ⌣

1 PROSCENIUM (end-staging)   *Stage Directions and Comments*

2 THRUST (horseshoe, three-fourths)

3 ARENA (four-sided)

4 TOTAL (island staging)

SECTION TEN

BUILD-UPS

When you reach this section, you are ready to combine characterization with structure and to concentrate on building a scene with logic, dramatic style, and theatrical intensity. Here are some quite advanced exercises to test your ability to concentrate on several levels at once while creating an original play. Have the instructor use the Grading Guide to record your progress at this point. Work to sustain your character in performance, keeping it fresh, spontaneous, and with awareness of the well-known theatrical tradition, "the miracle of the first time." This quality distinguishes theatre among all the arts and, more than anything else, raises acting from a craft.

1 Consistent Continuity Concentrate on the structure and story line as much as on your individual characterization. Stay in character while observing what each other one is doing, and build your own character's reactions on their contributions. Let your motivations be guided by the ensemble, as well as by your character's needs. Be sure you are able to share the scene, letting those who are momentarily carrying the action "take the spotlight," as it were, so that plot can unfold.

   a To really apply "consistent continuity," improvise a one-act play to last the entire session.

   b For more challenge, try to create plays of different styles: comedy, tragedy, sociodrama, domestic drama, farce, Absurdism. Get started with ideas by reading aloud together from current news clippings, excerpts from favorite novels, poems, letters, lyrics of songs old and new (each one can bring in his own selection, and the group can decide). Then discuss the dramatic possibilities: style, characters, setting. Finally, without "playwriting," stage it! You will be surprised and perhaps inspired at what ensemble concentration, imagination, and observation can produce.

2 Circle-Scenes These are quite popular among improvisational student actors. In a way they resemble the birth of a being.

   a Create a totally original character by the "circle of associates" method. One actor sits in the center of the playing area while three or four (no more) others walk around him, stopping a moment whenever one is moved to voice his relationship to the central person. The remarks must be brief, confined to establishing relationships and identities, without going into any action or plot outlining. Each succeeding speaker explains his character and relationship to the central figure in logical development from what has gone before but without referring to plot. All remarks are addressed directly to the central person, whose eyes remain closed during this expository circling and whose mind remains open to receive all the identities. He is like a piece of clay allowing itself to be molded by several sculptors into an image that is the product of their combined imaginations. He knows who he is only because of what they have said about his relationship to them. When it is your turn to play this central character, you will discover how your listening ability will be tested, and how your concentration and imagination will enable you to combine several suggestions into a consistent character.

Example: You are sitting as in a mental vacuum with your eyes closed. You hear Voice No. 1 address you by name and say, "You and I have always been close friends, but lately you have become rather cool toward me. I don't understand why, since we have shared every problem since childhood. Have I done something to upset you? Or are you tired of me? Has someone else entered your life that causes this distance between us?" In the silence that follows, you think about this person, your friend, and your past relationship. You are naturally curious about his concern, but you must wait to learn more about yourself before you can draw any conclusions.

Voice No. 2 speaks to you: "I don't know what you see in So-and-So (naming Voice No. 1) because you know he can't be trusted. You always were rather gullible, especially when someone flatters you. Who should know better than I, your own (husband? wife? brother? sister? mother? father? lover?)? I think it's time that you quit depending on So-and-So and broadened your circle of friends. But why should I expect you to listen to me? You never have, ever since that incident at the theatre." During the silence you try to understand your real relationship to Voice No. 2 and to recall "that incident at the theatre." You are divided in your loyalties between these two people, but you aren't yet sure why.

You listen, as Voice No. 3 addresses you with, "Hey, don't be so glum, chum. Your public wants to see you smiling, and if you want to retain me as your (agent? manager? director? producer?) you'd better put on that happy face. You never see me in low spirits, do you? For the past five years that we've worked together I've watched you change a lot—maybe you should try some of the stuff I use. But you're always so fussy about anything like that, aren't you?"

Now you begin to see your relationship to these three in terms of some kind of performance career, and a possible jealousy between Voices No. 1 and No. 2. Voice No. 3 adds another dimension with his superficial "happy talk" and temptations of artificial stimulants. Or is he really sincere? Does he offer you more than the other two? Must you make a selection among these three, or can you accept them all as equally beneficial to your life? And just how have you "changed a lot" in the past five years?

It helps if the actors use their real names at first, but in later Circle-Scenes fictitious names should be used. After everyone has identified himself, all but the central person move to the sidelines and remain seated in silence. There must be *no* "playwriting" or preplanning while waiting to appear.

b   One by one, each character, or antagonist, "pays a call" on the central person, the protagonist, whose life and identity have been fashioned by the remarks in the circle. Each of these "visits" is brief, a well-timed short conversation between the antagonist and the protagonist regarding the personal conflicts that became evident during the circle remarks. After each visitor leaves, the protagonist has a moment to himself in which he is obviously moved to a new level of understanding or confusion, as the case may be. The next visitor must move the plot along a little further. If the final visitor does not resolve the situation, the protagonist must do so. Again, there must be no preplanning on the order of visits or on the plot development. Reliance on natural wit and variety of personalities will help to balance any temptation to develop a melodrama or soap opera or to duplicate one's everyday life and acquaintances, which may be interesting to the actors but quite dull for observers. Strive for originality: remember how each one of the Six-Segments can be significantly different from your own.

c   A variation would be to have each visitor remain while the next one appears and adds to the conflict—similar to a type of transformation scene described earlier.

d   A more difficult variation would be to restrict the setting to a certain time or place suggested by the group or the instructor before starting the circle. Conversely, let the setting and time be determined by a spectator *after* the circling has been completed.

These variations of Circle-Scenes will help avoid the easy stereotyped setting of the protagonist's home. You will discover with the Circle-Scene exercise why it is perhaps the most challenging, and the most exciting, of all the exercises attempted so far, and why it serves as a practical summary of Part Three.

Part Four

Rehearsal Techniques

So far you have discovered several basic principles recurring throughout these exercises. Let us review them before applying them to the final step, the preparation of an accepted play for public performance.

1 For acting purposes, you can see yourself as a tripartite being consisting of body, mind, and emotion.

2 Only when all three are functioning in harmony, and in the proper proportion for the particular job, can you achieve satisfaction in your acting.

3 Through the process called "acting" you must discover a particular kind of truth, a freedom, a special sort of energy. Your awareness of this impetus flooding through you is conveyed to your audience in a warmth of conviction between actor and spectator. Then occurs that "willing suspension of disbelief" described by the English philosopher-poet Samuel Taylor Coleridge as the essence of theatre.

4 The effective use of your voice, an important component of "body" in the tripartite being, can best release the real you, manifesting both your emotional and imaginative life.

5 The controlled use of your body can manifest the physical presence of your own character in daily living or of a created character in a role onstage.

6 Improvisation can lead to the cultivation of total sensitivity, awareness, freedom.

SECTION ELEVEN

PLAY-UPS

Now then, in the advanced learning of acting techniques, rehearsal of a scene from a written script can serve as the most intensive type of discipline. The scene becomes a framework within which you must confine your concentration, imagination, and observation. Previously, you worked without any preconceived pattern so long as you were spontaneously creating the situation and dialogue to fit your characterization.

Now you may at first feel somewhat restricted by the playwright's words and action. That is because he has already created the character for you, although perhaps in only one dimension, and your first obligation is to understand that character through your director's interpretation of the play as a whole. Very well. But what does that leave for you to do as a creative actor?

Recall that, in many of the improvisational sketches, you were performing within some sort of framework and, rather than feeling limited, you were able to use it as a basis to employ your concentration, imagination, and observation. The same applies to building a character *within the framework* supplied by a playwright and a director. If you improvise on the information supplied by them, your character will be consistent in whatever situation the playwright describes and the director stages.

This consistency is retained because you have become aware of the truth of your character through your C.I.O. process. You can test the accuracy of this truth by placing your character in hypothetical situations not in the play, and observing his action and reaction. The most valuable result of having applied the techniques of improvisation in rehearsal will be the freshness and spontaneity, "the miracle of the first time," you experience in each performance.

1 Solo Read-and-Do Here's a method of learning scenes quickly and believably for rehearsals and/or auditions. Following our pattern of simple solo work leading to complex ensembles, these first exercises are to help you either learn a single speech from a play in which you might be cast or prepare for an audition scene in the future. (If the latter purpose is your present need, it would be best for you now to consult the Audition Scenes Guide, pp. 129-130. When you have made your cutting, you will be ready to come back to these next steps.)

a Read aloud through the whole excerpt, including any of the author's stage directions.

b Set the script aside and get on your feet at once. Improvise the scene from as much as you recall in that first oral reading. You will know when you have omitted an idea or action because of a breakdown in continuity and communication between your character and any others in the scene. *But*: you *must* muddle through somehow to the next point you can remember, even if it's only the last line! This is extremely important: keep going! To paraphrase an old theatre adage, "The scene must go on." You will presently appreciate the reason for this step.

c Go back to the script for another *oral* reading of the whole scene. That is, don't just find the spot(s) where you broke down, but learn the context of those spots by reading them as part of a whole. After you have done the second reading aloud (and don't try to get it letter-perfect—that is not the purpose at this time), put the script down, get up and improvise the scene again. The process of Read-and-Do is repeated—oral reading, then improvising—until you are sure of the sequence. That is why you must start from the beginning each time you read the scene or improvise it. You are learning only the *sequence of thoughts* in coordination with necessary action. You are not learning words in this step.

If you have been schooled in the method that insists on memorizing words before action begins, or on stumbling around with a script in hand trying to tie words and action together too soon, then you will have some difficulty understanding the improvisational approach to scene rehearsals. Just don't put a time limit on yourself at this point in your development. Follow these steps exactly, and the whole process will become clear to you as you do it. That, of course, will be much more beneficial than having someone tell you about it.

d Note that you are not concerned with subtleties of characterization at this point any more than you are with the playwright's exact words. But you will find in repeated improvisations of the scene that the words are beginning to come; you will be using less of your own vocabulary and more of the character's typical diction to express his thoughts in *his* way. So now you are ready to start working for accuracy as well as continuity.

Using one small file card (3" × 5" or 4" × 6") which you can hold in the palm of your hand, make up a cue card. In other words, go through each phrase of your speech and note the key word or words, without which there would be no sense, no message. You will select image words such as nouns, verbs, and adjectives rather than articles, prepositions, and conjunctions, which seldom carry the meat of an idea. Put these in proper sequence on your cue card (see sample cue cards, pp. 136 and 140), using only one side if possible. Have your instructor check your cue card before you use it.

e   Now read aloud your speech from the cue card; then compare your reading to the full script. (A tape recorder will help.) Correct any major omissions, and reread.

f   On your feet again, play the scene as word-perfect as possible with the cue card in hand, performing gestures and business the best you can while holding the cue card. Consult the card quickly and as infrequently as possible, but keep going.

g   Put the cue card aside and play through the scene without it. Perhaps one or two repeats of this step will be sufficient for you to learn the scene completely.

h   When you are quite sure of continuity, of all the ideas and action in sequence, start concentrating on your character. Use the Six-Segment Character Analysis worksheet from Part Three to "peel the orange" of this character so that the six segments are revealed. Have your instructor check it for thoroughness. Keep in mind that the time and place of the scene are additional influences, which will help to determine the age, physical presence, clothing and accessories, temperament, background, and general attitude your character will have. Seek the truth in terms of time and place as well as mental and physical makeup. Listen to what the playwright tells you in stage directions throughout the whole play, what others say about your character in their dialogue throughout the play, what your own character reveals about himself in word and deed. Obviously, you will have to reread the play several times to absorb all the needed information or intimations. This thorough reading will help you to avoid preconceptions, false assumptions, and stereotypes based on inadequate observation which have little to do with the truth of character, on or off stage.

i   As you play the scene, let your imagination be restricted only by the truth of your character, so that spontaneous reactions and natural mannerisms will develop. With each repetition of the scene, in private or for spectators, these traits will become more and more "characteristic"—more true to life.

j   Submit a complete Six-Segment Character Analysis to your instructor for approval before presentation of the scene.

2 Ensemble Read-and-Do   This method employs the same process for ensemble scene rehearsals as you used for your private rehearsals of a solo scene. However, since your director may not use this method in group or full-cast rehearsals, your first obligation is to become aware of his technique and follow his directions carefully. If you do not have frequent opportunity to use the improvisational approach at present rehearsals, perhaps you can experiment with it in preparing group scenes for acting class or with a few friends. Of course, there's always the possibility that you will be directing a scene or play yourself, and then you may put this method to the test.

Make up an excerpt script, as illustrated with the scene from *The Lower Depths* (pp. 137-139), but do not make a cue card condensation of it (see p. 140) until you are sure of the final casting.

a Casting an ensemble scene can be done through improvisation. First, read aloud together the complete scene, with no definite parts assigned. Then put the script down and let everyone participate in the first improvisation of the scene, muddling through despite breaks, as you did for your solo scene.

b Exchange parts, with no one repeating the same role, and read aloud from the script again. Get up and do another improvised run-through of the whole scene. Repeat this step until everyone has played every part at least once, regardless of gender.

c When you really appreciate each role's possibilities and importance in the scene, you can discuss final casting based on physical, vocal, and personal factors.

d Now is the time for each cast member to make his own cue card of the scene. An ensemble cue card will have to include key words from all the speeches in the scene, as well as entrance and exit action. (See sample, p. 140.)

e Of course, each cast member should submit a detailed autobiography of his character, using the Six-Segment Character Analysis Worksheet as a guide.

3 Scene Introductions An important part of presenting a single scene to an audience, whether solo or ensemble, is a clear and brief introduction to be delivered by one of the participants. If you are elected, include the following information in your introduction:

a State the title of the play in full, including "The" if it appears as the first word in published versions (*The Lower Depths, The Fantasticks, The Merchant of Venice*, and so forth). Remember that "the" is pronounced "thuh" except when it precedes a word beginning with a vowel, as in *The Only Way, The Old Mill*; then it is pronounced "thee."

b Give the full name of the playwright, pronouncing it correctly. It may be necessary to get advice on some foreign names, but the least we can do is learn the accepted Anglicized pronunciation.

c Pronounce correctly the names of the actors and their characters in the scene, and briefly identify the latter in relation to the plot or central characters.

d Give the act and scene, along with the time and place.

e A brief synopsis of the play's action to the moment of your scene is usually helpful, except in the case of a familiar scene from a well-known play. Even in this instance, the synopsis helps to get the audience into the mood and serves as a preparatory moment for the participants.

f When you have finished the introduction, give a slight bow and leave the playing area to allow a lapse of time and aesthetic distance to occur while you silently get into character. Some actors are able to do this merely by turning their backs to the audience as they think themselves into their roles, while others have to withdraw completely from sight, sit down, and meditate a few moments. Experienced actors often are able to go right from an introduction into a character with only a slight pause or a definite piece of well-planned movement or business. At any rate, keep your audience's needs in mind and don't make any transitions too abrupt. (This would include the closing effect also. When you stop the action, bow your head for a moment, hold the pose while the audience comprehends that it is over, and then leave the area with a composed, dignified exit. In that way the audience can still be thinking about the character rather than about you as a personality.)

g In delivering the introduction, bear in mind that it is you, not the character, who is talking with (not at) the audience. Therefore, take advantage of this one moment in the performance to be yourself, and don't let a dull reading of notes serve as your medium of communication. Look into the audience directly, have a pleasant smile, an informative tone, and feel that you are helping them to get ready for a worthwhile experience. Let's hope that, as a result of all these Play-Ups steps, it will be.

4 *Production Rehearsals* As stated earlier, some directors may follow the Read-and-Do exercises in rehearsing full-length plays and musicals as well as for workshop solo or ensemble scenes. For musicals, song lyrics may be improvised as prose until memorized, and then may be spoken as poems until the music is ready to be added.

a Each "French scene" of the production, whether play or musical, should be improvised as outlined in Play-Ups Exercise No. 2 under "Ensemble Read-and-Do," pp. 125-126. (A "French scene" is determined by each combination of characters onstage and is terminated by the exit or entrance of anyone—the traditional means of scene division in classic French drama.)

b When every scene of each act has been improvised, your director may have you run through the whole play without a pause, skipping minor details of blocking if they are still unclear to you. In this type of improvisational rehearsal, you as actor are still actively creating your role and blocking, but the director will be gradually and firmly setting the best moments of spontaneity into the total impression of the play. Allow for these moments, and work harmoniously to blend with the ensemble and the play's particular message being stressed in your production.

c When you have established your character, you will find it helpful to place him in situations different from those in the play, but logical for him to experience. These original variations can be on your own, or with other characters or the whole ensemble. Some directors use them as part of their warm-ups before the actual rehearsal begins. For example, Tom O'Horgan, who staged the original New York production of *Hair*, used such warm-ups for an improvised TV play about Leif Ericson in America, "The Tribe" by Paul Foster.*

Each rehearsal begins with actors' calisthenics. After a half-hour, O'Horgan steps in and quietly suggests creative group activities to the company. These can be as simple as asking the actors to form a circle, close their eyes, move away from the circle, and then grope their way back to a reforming of the circle. Or they can become enormously complex, with actors asked to imagine three colors, associate each with a specific sensation or vocal utterance, and to alternate between the three in some physical activity accomplished during the span of one breath.

Sometimes O'Horgan will ask the actors to extend their activity right into an improvisation that uses the dialogue of the play. Or as the director explains it, "I try to get the actors involved in an activity difficult enough to keep their minds and bodies interested in what they are doing. Then I attach the activity to an emotionalization that has something to do with the play."

Although such procedures stimulate the free creativity of the individual actors, the creativity is practiced with a constant awareness of the needs and responses of the rest of the group. Sometimes the actors will try to mirror the improvisations of one creator, but O'Horgan will keep shifting the creator role from one actor to another.

d   To test the consistency of your character, your director may wish to construct a rehearsal in the form of a "happening." That is, he will find ways to interrupt the scene, or to distract you with surprise elements in the form of irrelevant props or costume pieces. If your determination to be truthful is strong enough, none of these disruptions will annoy or amuse you, and you will continue to ignore them or adapt to them without faltering, with the cool poise of the professional.

e   When you and your director agree on your character, write a revised autobiography; you are merely a secretary, writing from your character's dictation, following his style of thought and diction. All the autobiographies may be read aloud to the ensemble, and taped or duplicated for future reference or revision. The publicity manager will certainly appreciate them as quotable items in "personality" advance releases.

f   Again, the interview can be very helpful for you to understand your own character as well as all the others in the play. The director can be the interviewer, and the occasion can be logically conceived as an extension of the plot.

*A description of his technique, entitled "Tom's Mix," by Henry Hewes appeared in the *Saturday Review* (July 12, 1969). Copyright 1969 Saturday Review, Inc. Reprinted by permission.

SECTION TWELVE

AUDITION SCENE GUIDE

Purpose

To prepare a short scene from a play which will enable you to demonstrate your techniques of characterization, projection of emotion, body control, use of stage space, and interpretative ability with the work of an established playwright.

Selection

First, consult lists of successful plays that have been recommended for reading by your instructors in past and present courses. Some of these lists may be among your class notes; others are found in literature texts or play anthologies. Do not restrict your selection to American or English authors but include translations of perhaps Russian, Italian, French, German, and Scandinavian plays.

When you have gathered these lists, scan them for familiar titles—perhaps plays of recent production in your area, or those that have appeared on television or in the movies. These will have stood the test of time and changing tastes because they deal with believable characters in human situations.

By checking casts of characters and lengths of speeches, narrow your selection to at least two plays, a comedy and a serious drama. You may have to scan several on the list before you're sure of their category of style. Read the plays of your choice quickly to absorb plot, setting, mood, theme, and characters. Compare the two plays in all these elements.

Carefully reread the play which presents the character who seems most to capture your interest and—most important—your understanding. Even if this character is unpleasant in every way, you may find him most fascinating and, strangely enough, worthy of your respect and sympathy. In other words, don't always be misled by the Romantic Lead because you'd like to identify your present personal life with that role. That's "soap opera" thinking and has little to do with your development as a *creative* actor. Remember what you've learned from the improvisational characters you've been creating. Which ones were the most interesting to you? On the other hand, avoid typecasting yourself in Villain or Rejected Lover or Martyr or Ideal Friend roles because of an unconfessed self-pity. That would be as limiting as always seeing yourself as Successful Lover or Beautiful Person because of an unpurged self-love.

After you've made your selection of play and character, set the alternate choice aside and begin work on the first one. Once you've completed a fair job of excerpting and learning an audition scene of a character you like, it will be easier to apply the same techniques to a second choice, and a third, and so on, until you've built a repertory of audition materials substantial enough to meet any occasion.

Script Preparation

Study the play to determine which are the key scenes of the character you will portray. Select that scene, or a series of speeches easily joined into one by introductory explanation or believable interpolations.

Ordinarily it is difficult for any single performer to handle dialogue with more than two people in a scene. In a solo audition scene, do not attempt to play anyone but your chosen character. "Place" the other person by directing your eyes and head to focus him in space, and be sure he does not shrink into the floor or into the seat of a chair, nor suddenly tower above you as an instant giant. We will know what the other person is like and what he says by the way you reply to him, or by your repeating his remarks as if for emphasis or clarification. Therefore, you can omit his speeches and turn yours into a sort of monologue, combining one or two long speeches with several short ones, even if you have to do some improvised interpolations. Your instructor will help you develop this technique. In the Cue Card samples section, compare the cutting of Linda's speech with the original passage from *Death of a Salesman* to see how other characters' speeches can be paraphrased or eliminated.

Now type out your scene in the way you will learn it. Double-space and leave wide margins to allow for write-in directions to yourself.

You will now be ready to apply the improvisational rehearsal techniques in the Play-Ups Exercise No. 1, "Solo Read-and Do" (p. 123).

SECTION THIRTEEN

SOME "CUTTING" REMARKS

Sometimes when you "cut" excerpts from a scene, you will have to make some alterations for vividness and conciseness. The following samples may be of help. Linda's speeches from Act I of Arthur Miller's *Death of a Salesman* have been extracted and combined into a monologue for a solo scene. You can see how many alterations were made from the original passage, yet how the intent and intensity are still retained. The excerpt has also been reduced to a Cue Card example, showing how key words are extracted for a small notecard to be held in your hand during improvisational rehearsals, as explained in Play-Ups 1-*d*, "Solo Read-and-Do" (p. 124).

A Scene from Act I, "Death of a Salesman," by Arthur Miller*

Biff Loman has returned home from out west. He is shocked at the mental deterioration of his father, Willy. Although Willy has worshipped Biff and sacrificed for him, Biff is alienated from his father. He and his brother Happy enjoy their mother, Linda, but this is not pleasing to her.

LINDA No. You can't just come to see me, because I love him. (*With a threat, but only a threat, of tears.*) He's the dearest man in the world to me, and I won't have anyone making him feel unwanted and low and blue. You've got to make up your mind now, darling, there's no leeway any more. Either he's your father and you pay him that respect, or else you're not to come here. I know he's not easy to get along with—nobody knows that better than me—but . . .

WILLY (*from the left, with a laugh*) Hey, hey, Biffo!

BIFF (*starting to go out after Willy*) What the hell is the matter with him? (*Happy stops him.*)

LINDA Don't—don't go near him!

---

*From *Death of a Salesman* by Arthur Miller. Copyright 1949 by Arthur Miller. Reprinted by permission of The Viking Press, Inc., and of Secker & Warburg.

BIFF Stop making excuses for him! He always, always wiped the floor with you. Never had an ounce of respect for you.

HAPPY He's always had respect for—

BIFF What the hell do you know about it?

HAPPY (*surlily*) Just don't call him crazy!

BIFF He's got no character—Charley wouldn't do this. Not in his own house—spewing out that vomit from his mind.

HAPPY Charley never had to cope with what he's got to.

BIFF People are worse off than Willy Loman. Believe me, I've seen them!

LINDA Then make Charley your father, Biff. You can't do that, can you? I don't say he's a great man. Willy Loman never made a lot of money. His name was never in the paper. He's not the finest character that ever lived. But he's a human being, and a terrible thing is happening to him. So attention must be paid. He's not to be allowed to fall into his grave like an old dog. Attention, attention must be finally paid to such a person. You called him crazy—

BIFF I didn't mean—

LINDA No, a lot of people think he's lost his—balance. But you don't have to be very smart to know what his trouble is. The man is exhausted.

HAPPY Sure!

LINDA A small man can be just as exhausted as a great man. He works for a company thirty-six years this March, opens up unheard-of territories to their trademark, and now in his old age they take his salary away.

HAPPY (*indignantly*) I didn't know that, Mom.

LINDA You never asked, my dear! Now that you get your spending money someplace else you don't trouble your mind with him.

HAPPY But I gave you money last—

LINDA Christmas time, fifty dollars! To fix the hot water it cost ninety-seven fifty! For five weeks he's been on straight commission, like a beginner, an unknown!

BIFF Those ungrateful bastards!

LINDA Are they any worse than his sons? When he brought them business, when he was young, they were glad to see him. But now his old friends, the old buyers that loved him so and always found some order to hand him in a pinch—they're all dead, retired. He used to be able to make six, seven calls a day in Boston. Now he takes his valises out of the car and puts them back and takes them out again and he's exhausted. Instead of walking he talks now. He drives seven hundred miles, and when he gets there no one knows him any more, no one welcomes him. And what goes through a man's mind, driving seven hundred miles home without having earned a cent? Why shouldn't he talk to himself? Why? When he has to go to Charley and borrow fifty dollars a week and pretend to me that it's his pay? How long can that go on? How long? You see what I'm sitting here and waiting for? And you tell me he has no character? The man who never worked a day but for your benefit? When does he get the medal for that? Is this his reward—to turn around at the age of sixty-three and find his sons, who he loved better than his life, one a philandering bum—

HAPPY Mom!

LINDA That's all you are, my baby! (*To Biff*) And you! What happened to the love you had for him? You were such pals! How you used to talk to him on the phone every night! How lonely he was till he could come home to you.

BIFF All right, Mom. I'll live here in my room, and I'll get a job. I'll keep away from him, that's all.

LINDA No, Biff. You can't stay here and fight all the time.

BIFF He threw me out of this house, remember that.

LINDA Why did he do that? I never knew why.

BIFF Because I know he's a fake and he doesn't like anybody around who knows!

LINDA Why a fake? In what way? What do you mean?

BIFF Just don't lay it all at my feet. It's between me and him—that's all I have to say. I'll chip in from now on. He'll settle for half my pay check. He'll be all right. I'm going to bed. (*He starts for the stairs.*)

LINDA He won't be all right.

BIFF (*turning on the stairs, furiously*) I hate this city and I'll stay here. Now what do you want?

LINDA He's dying, Biff. (*Happy turns quickly to her, shocked.*)

BIFF (*after a pause*) Why is he dying?

LINDA He's been trying to kill himself.

BIFF (*with great horror*) How?

LINDA I live from day to day.

BIFF What're you talking about?

LINDA Remember I wrote you that he smashed up the car again? In February?

BIFF Well?

LINDA The insurance inspector came. He said that they have evidence. That all these accidents in the last year—weren't—weren't accidents.

HAPPY How can they tell that? That's a lie.

LINDA It seems there's a woman . . . (*She takes a breath as . . .*)

BIFF (*sharply but contained*) What woman?

LINDA . . . and this woman . . .

(*simultaneously*)

LINDA What?

BIFF Nothing. Go ahead.

LINDA What did you say?

BIFF Nothing. I just said what woman?

HAPPY What about her?

LINDA Well, it seems she was walking down the road and saw his car. She says that he wasn't driving fast at all, and that he didn't skid. She says he came to that little bridge, and then deliberately smashed into the railing, and it was only the shallowness of the water that saved him.

BIFF Oh, no, he probably just fell asleep again.

LINDA I don't think he fell asleep.

BIFF Why not?

LINDA Last month . . . (*with great difficulty*) Oh, boys, it's so hard to say a thing like this! He's just a big stupid man to you, but I tell you there's more good in him than in many other people. (*She chokes, wipes her eyes.*) I was looking for a fuse. The lights blew out, and I went down the cellar. And behind the fuse box—it happened to fall out—was a length of rubber pipe—just short.

HAPPY No kidding?

LINDA There's a little attachment on the end of it. I knew right away. And sure enough, on the bottom of the water heater there's a new little nipple on the gas pipe.

HAPPY (*angrily*) That—jerk.

BIFF Did you have it taken off?

LINDA I'm—I'm ashamed to. How can I mention it to him? Every day I go down and take away that little rubber pipe. But, when he comes home, I put it back where it was. How can I insult him that way? I don't know what to do. I live from day to day, boys. I tell you, I know every thought in his mind. It sounds so old-fashioned and silly, but I tell you he put his whole life into you and you've turned your backs on him. (*She is bent over in the chair, weeping, her face in her hands.*) Biff, I swear to God! Biff, his life is in your hands!

A Cutting from Act I, "Death of a Salesman"*

LINDA You can't just come to see me, because I love him. (*With a threat, but only a threat, of tears.*) He's the dearest man in the world to me, and I won't have anyone making him feel unwanted and low and blue. You've got to make up your mind now, darling, there's no leeway any more. Either he's your father and you pay him that respect, or else

*Brackets indicate paraphrased interpolations for continuity.

you're not to come here. I know he's not easy to get along with—nobody knows that better than me—but . . . don't—don't go near him! I don't say he's a great man. Willy Loman never made a lot of money. His name was never in the paper. He's not the finest character that ever lived. But he's a human being, and a terrible thing is happening to him. So attention must be paid. He's not to be allowed to fall into his grave like an old dog. Attention, attention must be finally paid to such a person. You called him crazy—a lot of people think he's lost his—balance. But you don't have to be very smart to know what his trouble is. The man is exhausted. A small man can be just as exhausted as a great man. He works for a company thirty-six years this March, opens up unheard-of territories to their trademark, and now in his old age they take his salary away. [I know you didn't know that]—you never asked, my dear! Now that you get your spending money someplace else you don't trouble your mind with him. Oh yes, you gave me money—last Christmas time! Fifty dollars! To fix the hot water it cost ninety-seven fifty! For five weeks he's been on straight commission, like a beginner, an unknown! [Why call them ungrateful?] Are they any worse than his sons? When he brought them business, when he was young, they were glad to see him. But now his old friends, the old buyers that loved him so and always found some order to hand him in a pinch—they're all dead, retired. He used to be able to make six, seven calls a day in Boston. Now he takes his valises out of the car and puts them back and takes them out again and he's exhausted. Instead of walking he talks now. He drives seven hundred miles, and when he gets there no one knows him any more, no one welcomes him. And what goes through a man's mind, driving seven hundred miles home without having earned a cent? Why shouldn't he talk to himself? Why? When he has to go to Charley and borrow fifty dollars a week and pretend to me that it's his pay? How long can that go on? How long? You see what I'm sitting here and waiting for? And you tell me he has no character? The man who never worked a day but for your benefit? When does he get the medal for that? Is this his reward—to turn around at the age of sixty-three and find his sons, who he loved better than his life, one a philandering bum—That's all you are, my baby! (*To Biff*) And you! What happened to the love you had for him? You were such pals! How you used to talk to him on the phone every night! How lonely he was till he could come home to you! No, Biff. You can't stay here and fight all the time. [Yes, he threw you out of this house. I remember.] Why did he do that? I never knew why. [A fake, you say?] Why a fake? In what way? What do you mean? [All right, so it's between you and him. But even if you chip in with half your pay check . . .] He won't be all right. He's dying, Biff. He's been trying to kill himself. I live from day to day. Remember that I wrote you that he smashed up the car again? In February? The insurance inspector came. He said that they have evidence. That all these accidents in the last year—weren't—weren't—accidents. It seems there's a woman . . . (*she takes a breath*) . . . What? What did you say? Well, it seems she was walking down the road and saw his car. She says that he wasn't driving fast at all, and that he didn't skid. She says he came to that little bridge, and then deliberately smashed into the railing, and it was only the shallowness of the water that saved him. [No,] I don't think he fell asleep. Last month . . . (*with great difficulty*) Oh, boys, it's so hard to say a thing like this! He's just a big stupid man to you, but I tell you there's more good in him than in many other people. (*She chokes, wipes her eyes.*) I was looking for a fuse. The lights blew out, and I went down the cellar. And behind the fuse box—it happened to fall out—was a length of rubber pipe—just short. There's a little attachment on the end of it. I knew right away. And sure enough, on the bottom of the water heater there's a new little nipple on the gas pipe. [Take it off? No—] I'm—I'm ashamed to. How can I mention it to him? Every day I go down and take away that little rubber pipe. But, when he comes home I put it back where it was. How can I insult him that way? I don't know what to do. I live from day to day, boys. I tell you, I know every thought in his mind. It sounds old-fashioned and silly, but I tell you he put his whole life into you and you've turned your backs on him. (*She is bent over in the chair, weeping, her face in her hands.*) Biff, I swear to God! Biff, his life is in your hands!

A Cue Card for Linda's Monologue, Act I, "Death of a Salesman"*

Can't come—see me—love him. Dearest man—won't have—feel unwanted—. Make up mind—no leeway. Your father—respect—not come. Not easy—better than me—don't go near. Don't say great man—Willy Loman—money. Name—paper. Not finest character. Human being—terrible thing—. Attention. Not allowed—grave—old dog. Attention, attention—paid—person. Crazy—people—balance. Smart—trouble. Exhausted. Small man—exhausted—great man. Works—company— 36 years—territories—trademark—old age—salary away. Didn't know— never asked. Spending money—trouble your mind—. Money—last Christmas—Fifty—hot water—$97.50. 5 weeks—commission—beginner, unknown. Ungrateful? worse than sons? Business—young—glad see him. Old friends—buyers—loved order to hand him—dead—retired. Used to—six, seven calls—Boston. Valises—car—puts back—takes out—exhausted. Walking—talks. Drives 700 miles—no one knows— welcomes—. Goes thru—mind—700 miles—cent? Talk to himself? Why? Charley—borrow 50—pretend—pay? How long—go on? How long? Sitting here—waiting for? No character? Never worked—benefit? Medal? Reward—63—sons—loved—bum—all you are—. Love for him? Pals! Talk—phone—every night. Lonely—home—you. No Biff. Can't stay— fight. Threw out. Why? Never knew. Fake? Why fake? mean? Between

---

*Note that only key words are extracted, consecutively, with no stage directions.

you, him. Half pay check. Won't be all right. Dying. Kill himself. Day to day. Smashed car? February? Insurance. Evidence. Accidents—weren't. Woman. What? Walking—road—car. Fast. Skid. Bridge—smashed railing—shallowness—saved. Asleep. Last month—hard to say—big stupid man—more good. Fuse. Lights blew—cellar. Fuse box—fall—pipe—attachment. Knew. Bottom water heater—nipple—pipe. Ashamed. Mention? Every day—pipe. Home—put it back. Insult? Don't know. Day to day. Every thought—. Old-fashioned, silly—whole life—turned backs. Biff—swear God—life—hands.

A Scene from Act I, "The Lower Depths," by Maxim Gorky*

The setting is a cave-like cellar of a slum tenement in Moscow at the turn of the Century. As the play opens, the occupants of this miserable sleeping-room are The Baron, Kvashnya (a vendor of meatpies), Bubnoff (a cap-maker), Satine (a gambler), Kleshtch (a locksmith), Nastya (a streetwalker). It is an early spring morning . . . (Later: Anna, Actor enter scene.)

THE BARON   And then?

KVASHNYA   No, my dear, said I, keep away from me with such proposals. I've been through it all, you see—and not for a hundred baked lobsters would I marry again!

BUBNOFF (*to Satine*)   What are you grunting about?
(*Satine keeps on grunting.*)

KVASHNYA   Why should I, said I, a free woman, my own mistress, enter my name into somebody else's passport and sell myself into slavery—no! Why—I wouldn't marry a man even if he were an American prince!

KLESHTCH   You lie!

KVASHNYA   Wha-at?

KLESHTCH   You lie! You're going to marry Abramka . . .

THE BARON (*snatching the book out of Nastya's hand and reading the title*)   "Fatal Love" . . . (*laughs*).

NASTYA (*stretching out her hand*)   Give it back—give it back! Stop fooling!
(*The Baron looks at her and waves the book in the air.*)

KVASHNYA (*to Kleshtch*)   You crimson goat, you—calling me a liar! How dare you be so rude to me?

THE BARON (*hitting Nastya on the head with the book*)   Nastya, you little fool!

*Translated from the Russian by Jennie Covan, as reprinted in *Fifteen Famous European Plays* by Random House, Inc., New York, 1943.

NASTYA (*reaching for the book*)   Give it back!

KLESHTCH   Oh—what a great lady . . . but you'll marry Abramka just the same—that's all you're waiting for . . .

KVASHNYA   Sure! Anything else? You nearly beat your wife to death!

KLESHTCH   Shut up, you old bitch! It's none of your business!

KVASHNYA   Ho-ho! can't stand the truth, can you?

THE BARON   They're off again! Nastya, where are you?

NASTYA (*without lifting her head*)   Hey—go away!

[*With the appearance of a new character, a new French scene begins.*]

ANNA (*putting her head through the curtains of her bed*)   The day has started. For God's sake, don't row!

KLESHTCH   Whining again!

ANNA   Every blessed day . . . let me die in peace, can't you?

BUBNOFF   Noise won't keep you from dying.

KVASHNYA (*walking up to Anna*)   Little Mother, how did you ever manage to live with this wretch?

ANNA   Leave me alone—get away from me . . .

KVASHNYA   Well, well! You poor soul . . . how's the pain in the chest—any better?

THE BARON   Kvashnya! Time to go to market . . .

KVASHNYA   We'll go presently. (*To Anna*) Like some hot dumplings?

ANNA   No, thanks. Why should I eat?

KVASHNYA   You must eat. Hot food—good for you! I'll leave you some in a cup. Eat them when you feel like it. Come on sir! (*To Kleshtch*) You evil spirit! (*Goes into kitchen.*)

ANNA (*coughing*)   Lord, Lord . . .

THE BARON (*painfully pushing forward Nastya's head*)   Throw it away—little fool!

NASTYA (*muttering*)   Leave me alone—I don't bother you . . .
(*The Baron follows Kvashnya, whistling.*)

[*With the exit of two characters, the second French scene ends, a third begins.*]

SATINE (*sitting up in his bunk*)   Who beat me up yesterday?

BUBNOFF   Does it make any difference who?

SATINE   Suppose they did—but why did they?

BUBNOFF   Were you playing cards?

SATINE   Yes!

BUBNOFF   That's why they beat you.

SATINE   Scoundrels!

[*With the entrance of The Actor into the action, a fourth French scene begins.*]

THE ACTOR (*raising his head from the top of the stove*)   One of these days they'll beat you to death!

SATINE   You're a jackass!

THE ACTOR   Why?

SATINE   Because a man can die only once!

THE ACTOR (*after a silence*)   I don't understand—

KLESHTCH   Say! You crawl from that stove—and start cleaning house! Don't play the delicate primrose!

THE ACTOR   None of your business!

KLESHTCH   Wait till Vassilisa comes—she'll show you whose business it is!

THE ACTOR   To hell with Vassilisa! Today is the Baron's turn to clean . . . Baron!

[*With the re-appearance of The Baron, the fifth French scene begins.*]

(*The Baron comes from the kitchen.*)

THE BARON   I've no time to clean . . . I'm going to market with Kvashnya.

THE ACTOR   That doesn't concern me. Go to the gallows if you like. It's your turn to sweep the floor just the same—I'm not going to do other people's work . . .

THE BARON   Go to blazes! Nastya will do it. Hey there—fatal love! Wake up! (*Takes book away from Nastya.*)

NASTYA (*getting up*)   What do you want? Give it back to me! You scoundrel! And that's a nobleman for you!

THE BARON (*returning the book to her*)   Nastya! Sweep the floor for me—will you?

NASTYA (*goes to kitchen*)   Not so's you'll notice it!

[*With Nastya's exit and Kvashnya's re-entrance the sixth French scene begins.*]

KVASHNYA (*to the Baron through the kitchen door*)   Come on—you! They don't need you! Actor! You were asked to do it, and now you go ahead and attend to it—it won't kill you . . .

THE ACTOR   It's always I . . . I don't understand why . . .

Ensemble Cue Card for Opening of "The Lower Depths"*

1 *Baron, Kvashnya, Bubnoff, Satine, Kleshtch, Nastya*
Then? — No — keep away — proposals — through it — lobsters — marry again.

Grunting?—Free woman—mistress—passport—slavery—marry American prince.

Lie—Abramka—Fatal Love—give back—fooling—goat—liar—rude? Little fool—give back—great lady—Abramka—waiting for—best wife—shut up—your business—truth?

Off again—Nastya?—go away—(*enter Anna*)

2 *Anna, with others as in #1*
Day started—row—whining—every blessed day—die in peace—noise—Little mother—live—wretch—leave alone—poor soul—pain—better?

Kavshnya — market — presently — dumplings? — no — why eat? — hot food—cup—feel like—Come—evil spirit—Lord—Throw away—fool—leave alone—bother . . . (*exit Kvashnya, Baron*)

3 *Bubnoff, Satine, Kleshtch, Nastya*
Beat me — difference? — why — cards? — yes — beat you — Scoundrels—(*enter Actor*)

4 *Actor, with others as in #3*
Days—beat to death—jackass—why?—die only once—don't understand—

Crawl—cleaning—delicate primrose—none business—Vassilisa comes—whose business—hell with—Baron's turn—Baron! (*enter Baron*)

5 *Baron, with others as in #4*
No time—market with Kvashnya—doesn't concern—gallows—turn to sweep—other people's work—blazes—Nastya—fatal love—wake—what want?—give back—scoundrel—nobleman!—sweep for me—notice it! (*exit Nastya, enter Kvashnya*)

6 Come on—don't need—Actor—asked—go ahead—attend—kill you—always I—don't understand . . .

---

*Note that entrances and exits are included with key words from all speeches.

SECTION FOURTEEN

IMPROVISATIONAL SHOWS

Purpose

You may feel that some of your exercises, ensemble scenes, and rehearsal techniques may be worthy of public presentation. If you think that a show built on improvisations would be important to your development as an actor, and if your group agrees, why not? Just keep in mind that any public staging is primarily to entertain an audience, not just for the fun of the performers. The Second City troupe originating in Chicago some years ago and more recently The Committee in San Francisco and Los Angeles have treated improvisational theatre purely as a form of commercial entertainment, not as an educational or therapeutic exercise for classroom or laboratory. These professional troupes have, to a certain extent, succeeded in their purpose, depending on audience ingenuity in dreaming up unusual ideas, and the performers sustained concentration, imagination, and keen observations of the world around them.

Style

Not all improvisations are designed for amusement. Quite serious improvisational moments can be effectively introduced into otherwise conventionally structured plays. The La Mama company from America was reviewed at an Edinburgh Festival by Harold Hobson, London drama critic for the international daily newspaper *The Christian Science Monitor*:

In a designedly revolutionary drama, "Tom Paine," periods were set aside for the company to discuss selected aspects of revolutionary activity. These topics were suggested by the author, Paul Foster. To this extent their scope was limited, but, since they were given some form and definition, they did not wander off into uncontrolled vagueness. Nevertheless they revealed how difficult improvisation may be. Even though they were given particular subjects to discuss, the company, at Edinburgh at any rate, discussed them only haltingly.[*]

[*]From *The Christian Science Monitor* (February 28, 1970). By permission.

A group of California college students had a similar experience when they staged a semi-improvised interpretation of Shakespeare's controversial comedy, *The Merchant of Venice.* During certain climactic moments they suddenly stopped the action to discuss the themes which they felt Shakespeare had raised in the play: prejudice, bigotry, and hypocrisy of both the Jewish and Christian characters. At each performance these interpolations varied in length and depth, but they invariably grew to such heated intensity that the audiences, although shocked at the unconventional interruptions, and at the sight of actors suddenly becoming real people, actually seemed to appreciate the play more as a contemporary comment than as a revived museum piece. Of course, a few purists in each audience were offended at such liberties being taken with The Bard, but they usually agreed, during the open discussion with the cast following each performance, that the jolting had been good for them, and that prejudice comes in many forms.

This illustration re-emphasizes the point that public improvisation is most effective when it evokes direct audience involvement in some way, and when the performers display wit, wisdom, and versatility in handling current issues.

Originality

Perhaps your group will discover new ways to use the old, old techniques of improvisation, whether for public or personal benefit. For example, you might experiment with a video-tape recorder or movie-making outfit and film some improvised satires on current TV features (talk shows, celebrity or sidewalk interviews, repetitive commercials, contradictory newscasts, daytime serials, situation comedies, or old movies). Then try editing and splicing the best ones, or even flash rapid-fire excerpts from each (as a series of "vaudeville" sight-gags) into a thematic program worth showing to invited audiences—who might even suggest that you tour it to clubs and schools, which would certainly be a boost to your public relations department.

Direction

In a classroom or studio, the "director" of an improvisation might well be you as a member of a spectator group awaiting your turn to perform. If so, in no sense will you dictate the interpretation of a sketch or exercise. You merely state the situation and/or characters to be developed, regulate the number of persons participating, and sometimes specify the length of each scene.

You might keep in mind how one group of London students organized themselves to present public improvisational shows. They had a manager, but not a stage director. Calling themselves the Incognito

Theatregroup, they shared expenses in order to be part of the 1968 Edinburgh Festival. The manager arranged rehearsals and bookings, but did no artistic directing. In performance, the individual actors seemed to become their own directors, while for each show they elected one of the company to serve as master of ceremonies. This person introduced the cast informally to the audience, ran the sequence of sketches, encouraged audience contributions, and just before each scene he selected the actors to perform, handle props or lighting, or to join the audience. But he never offered even a hint of interpretation or instruction.

You may be interested in how a teacher at a Roman Catholic high school in Texas applied improvisational directing techniques to liberate his students from inhibitions and self-consciousness. William A. McWhirter described him in *Life*:

Joseph M. Gonzales, alias Brother Alexis. . . a member of the 17th Century teaching order of Christian Brothers. . . is willing to let anyone help him direct and, like volunteer firemen, the amateurs appear nightly to whisper stage notes in his ear. Alexis does not even go up on the stage, but sits hulking like a cardinal in the rear ranges of the auditorium. The rehearsals seem to be free-form animation, a number of parts putting themselves together, and all that is apparent are the vibrations. "How do you see it?" he keeps asking the actors. "How would you play it? Do you like it this way? Are you being natural? Go ahead, don't do what I tell you to do, look foolish, make a mistake . . ." . . . The brother has allowed and, at times, even forced his students to be free—free to probe, interpret, and react . . . His method is to create a vacuum where anyone is free to do what he wishes—and obligated to do something against the void.*

Casting

If your group decides to hold auditions for an improvisational show, or if you yourself wish to try out for such a production in the future, your experience with the exercises in this handbook may be of more help to you than your repertory of ready-made audition scenes. In some avant-garde troupes of semi- or full-professional theatre, a director may employ surprisingly effective means to select a cast for a unique production, one which might be from a conventionally memorized script, or totally improvised, or a blending of both techniques. To help you become aware of and to prepare for these types of auditions, here are excerpts from an article on the subject.

*From *Life* (January 31, 1969). © 1969 Time Inc. Reprinted by permission.

Casting the Non-Play*

Gordon Rogoff has said of the current theatrical trend that "today's inclination is not as much toward the perfect text, something finished, unbending, or marbleized, as it is toward the collaboratively suggestive, improvisational architecture of a fluid, open text." Directors influenced by such new theatre ensembles as Cafe La Mama, The Open Theatre, Theatre of the Ridiculous, The Living Theatre, and the plethora of recent off-off Broadway experimenters, have begun to think in terms of presenting an evening of theatre consisting of short, non-narrative works: songs, dances, burlesques, improvisations, acrobatics, magic, clownery, film clips, and psychedelic mixed media bombardment of the senses. They are forming ensembles dedicated to the non-play . . .

Traditionally, actors are selected for a company on the basis of closeness to the physical and vocal type of the *dramatis personae* of the plays scheduled for the season. Type casting prevails, and those actors who seem "right" for the parts available are given a series of readings, the best readers usually winning out. This practice is not feasible for the director of the non-play since he is often forming an ensemble without having decided on the evening's program. (He could still advertise an evening of "provoking improvisations and theatre pieces" in advance publicity releases, which is vague enough to allow the creation of the program during rehearsals.)

The first step in casting an ensemble for the non-play is to devote a good portion of the initial interview to putting the auditioning actor at ease. The director engages him in a cordial chat about his background, interest, and aspirations, thus building his confidences and trust . . .

When the director feels the actor is comfortable enough to start the second phase of the audition, he may put the actor to work on a simple improvisation. The improvisation, the director can explain, is non-verbal and built upon the imaginative use of small objects . . . When the actor is in the midst of his pantomime he is given a third and fourth unrelated object (perhaps a plant or monkey wrench) and asked to incorporate them. Using the new objects tests his willingness to alter the story spontaneously. The exercise also indicates something of his intelligence, because he must find a logical thread that ties unrelated objects together . . .

After the improvisation is over, and if the director is pleased with the results, the actor is asked to read a sheet of non-descript sentences aloud. It is the actor's task to find or give meaning to this text.

A simple one-action improvisation is given to the actor. The exercise requires two actors, each presumably having reached the same plateau in separate auditions . . . The two actors are told where the improvised situation is to take place . . . The actors are then told their objectives. If

*Excerpts from "Casting the Non-Play," by Michael E. Rutenberg *Players,* The Magazine of American Theatre (April-May 1969). Reprinted by permission of *Players* and the author.

Part Four

one or both are inexperienced, the director should not use the word "objective" as it will confuse an untrained actor . . .

During the improvisation the director watches to see how well the actors carry out his suggestions. Are they playing their objectives? Is the activity continued, and is it truthful and fully developed in terms of sense memory techniques? Is a distinct relationship evolving out of the encounter? Do they listen to each other? Have they let the environment and the weather affect their behavior? . . . When the improvisation is over, or stopped by the director, he should ask them to repeat it again—this time offering an *adjustment* which will alter the circumstances. He may propose that one character now introduce a *physical state* as his adjustment . . .

In order that both display their own personalities, the actors should be discouraged from playing "characters . . ." If one of the actors shies away from direct personal involvement and seems reluctant to use his own name, he is not ready to assume the actor's responsibility which is *to be private in public*. The improvisation also tests the actor's willingness to depend on his partner. Since there is no script he must listen to the other actor in order to know what comes next. Learning to play for one's partner is essential in the training of actors for participation in the non-play ensemble . . .

At the second audition two different returning actors are brought together . . . they are given a short scene to read. It may be published or original material, but short enough to be read twice through in a few minutes. When they have finished reading the script they are told to approach it in the same manner they did the earlier improvisation. They are asked to play an objective, an activity (at least attempt to indicate an activity with the book in hand), a relationship, and a physical state. The director tells them where the scene takes place. . . .

When the scene is finished the actors are asked to make specific adjustments . . . The director might ask the actor to play the scene as if he were in a huge balloon, or taking a warm bath, or walking about in a pool of molasses. If the actors successfully fulfill their new adjustments, they should be called to a third and final audition and told to bring a record of their favorite vocalist. The actors are also asked to bring leotards or other appropriate gymnastic attire.

The third audition is the most difficult because it asks the actor to be his most uninhibited. The audition is concerned with accomplishing a series of physical and animal exercises . . . When the actor arrives, a few minutes are devoted to relaxation exercises. For example, the actor is asked to lie down on the floor. Then he is instructed to tense his toes for fifteen seconds and then relax them. Each major muscle group is then tensed and relaxed until the actor feels comfortable . . . After the relaxation exercises music is begun, and the actor is asked to dance to it. The music (acid rock is recommended) should stimulate the actor to let loose and dance as wildly as possible. It should be stressed that this portion of the audition process is paramount, because so much of the new ensemble work is physical. The director should check the actor's styling, his grace and co-ordination as he dances to the music . . . The actor is told to wear earphones and sing and dance along with the record. The exercise allows the director to hear how the actor would sound with the ensemble. It also gives the actor courage to sing out loud so that the director can test his stamina and breath control as well as his singing voice.

When the song and dance exercise is finished the actor is given the opportunity to try certain physical stunts . . . If he is unwilling or can't do the physical exercise, it is highly likely that he will hold back and not extend himself to the limits of the various roles he will have to play during one evening of non-play theatre. Ability to react fully to an emotional experience or state requires that the actor be in excellent physical and emotional condition.

The director now suggests certain animal improvisations that will help further reveal the actor's inhibitions and vocal range. This improvisation can take the form of a group exercise with a few of the finalists participating. The director may either assign each actor an animal or (preferably) allow him to portray his own favorite. Much can be learned about an actor's personality from the animal with which he identi- fies . . . Next, each actor plays an objective (for example, to protect his drinking area), an activity (drinking, or washing, or playing), develops a relationship to the other animals, and concentrates on a physical state . . . If the actor is truly involved with the animal life of his character, he will forget about "correct" vocal production, keep his throat open, and display an unobstructed series of sounds that tell the director his vocal strength and range. The exercise also shows the degree to which the actor is able to observe and imitate life around him. When the exercise is over, or stopped by the director, the actors are instructed to retain the animal characteristics as they re-read the scene used at their second audition.

If the director still needs a further test of the actor's talent, he has the opportunity to put each finalist through an *affective* or *emotion memory* exercise. This exercise should be done privately with all other finalists waiting in an adjoining area . . . It is not at all necessary for the auditioning actor to have to attempt recreating a moment of terror or hysteria through affective memory . . . Just ask him to talk about when he last had an uproarious time, or relate that moment when something truly inspiring happened to him. The director could, if he wishes, ask the actor to talk about a rather sad experience without suggesting that he search his memory for moments of utter desolation . . . The director then asks him to incorporate the feelings of the affective memory into the reading of the script used earlier. The actor who is able to color the reading with the feelings aroused by the emotion memory is one the director wants, because the art of acting is the art of calling upon past experiences which have been revitalized by spontaneous and open response to present stimuli. . . .

To have a successful ensemble for the theatre the director must find a way of determining what these procedures are designed to search out—first, the ability of the actor to build imaginatively from a few key stimuli; second the actor's willingness to become interested in the pursuit of situational objectives; third, the actor's freedom and willingness to be private in public; fourth, the actor's responsiveness to outside direction; fifth, the actor's stamina, physical control, and vocal range; sixth, the actor's fluency in emotional recall and projection.

Conclusion

You can see that the scope and application of improvisation are unlimited in today's theatre. If you are a reader of avant-garde theatre publications like *The Drama Review* or *After Dark*, or of the drama critics of major periodicals, some of whom we've quoted, you have no doubt become aware of the increasing interest in improvisational theatre. Perhaps you will want to use the last pages of this handbook to start a collection of clippings on the subject. If so, be sure to note the publication and date of each article so that you will be able to keep this book as an active and contemporary guide on the art of improvisation as it affects your personal development in theatre.

Remember, whenever you improvise, always be wise: there is no substitute for taste, for integrity, for artistry, in reaching and pleasing your audience. After all, these people are the reason for your efforts, aren't they? Through the centuries the audience has demanded that certain disciplines be followed for the sake of theatrical communication, whether improvised or memorized. In the case of memorized productions, you the actor can use improvisational techniques only in the rehearsal period, as an effective means of discovering the truth about your character through a total awareness of all possible influences on that character. But this discovery must be within the framework established by the playwright's words and the director's interpretation of them. Only then can you as the actor become the medium of communication of truth to the individual spectators that make up your audience. The sequence then is playwright-to-director-to-actor-to-spectator. When you successfully apply the ancient disciplines of the stage actor's art, you can personally experience that circular response which occurs between you and the audience at the moment of communication. But it will take a lifetime of learning, guided by competent coaches and the constant study of great plays and writings about the living theatre, to master these disciplines for the sake of your audience.

Samuel Johnson, though not an actor himself, spoke for all of us years ago as he dedicated London's famous Drury Lane Theatre:

The Drama's Laws the Drama's Patrons give;
And we who live to please, *must* please—to live!

CURTAIN

Selected Readings

Here are a few books related to improvisational acting and stage techniques. Consult their bibliographies, as well as local libraries, for other works and new publications on the subject so that you can develop your own reading list.

Improvisation

These books are basic to a background and understanding of improvisational acting:

Hodgson, John, and Richards, Ernest. *Improvisation: Discovery and Creativity in Drama*. London: Methuen and Co., Ltd.; New York: Barnes and Noble, Inc., 1966. 209 pp.

Nicoll, Allardyce. *The World of Harlequin*. Cambridge, England: University Press, 1963. 242 pp.

Smith, Winifred. *The Commedia dell 'Arte*. New York: Benjamin Blom, 1964. 338 pp.

Spolin, Viola. *Improvisation for the Theatre: A Handbook of Teaching and Directing Techniques*. Evanston, Ill.: Northwestern University Press, 1963. 395 pp.

General Acting Techniques

These sources provide guidance in fundamental skills necessary for any style of stage acting.

Albright, Hardie. *Acting: The Creative Process*. Belmont, Calif.: Dickenson Publishing Co., Inc., 1967. 287 pp.

Blunt, Jerry. *Stage Dialects*. San Francisco: Chandler Publishing Co., 1967.

———. *Stage Dialects on Tape*. San Francisco: Chandler Publishing Co., 1967 (Distributors: Science Research Associates, Inc., 259 East Erie St., Chicago, Ill. 60611). Three tapes to accompany manual: (1) Phonetic Alphabet, Japanese, Brooklynese, American Southern; (2) Standard English, Cockney, Irish, Scots; (3) French, Italian, German, Russian.

Challgren, Patricia, and Kennedy, Belle. *The Busy Speaker's Pocket Practice Book*. New York: Samuel French, 1959. 176 pp.

Morosco, Selma Paley, and Lounsbury, Athea. *Stage Technique Made Easy*. New York: M. S. Mill Cox, 1942. 94 pp.

Seyler, Athene, and Haggard, Stephen. *The Craft of Comedy.* New York: Theatre Arts, Inc., 1946. 104 pp.

Great Actors

These sources contain the opinions and theories of some of the world's greatest actors, past and present.

Burton, Hal (ed.). *Great Acting*. London: British Broadcasting Corporation, 1967. 192 pp. Interviews with Laurence Olivier, Sybil Thorndike, Ralph Richardson, Peggy Ashcroft, Michael Redgrave, Edith Evans, John Gielgud, Noel Coward.

Duerr, Edwin. *The Length and Depth of Acting*. New York: Holt, Rinehart and Winston, 1963. 590 pp.

Funke, Lewis, and Booth, John E. *Actors Talk About Acting*. 2 vols. New York: Avon Book Division, The Hearst Corporation, 1961.

————. *Famous Actors Talk on Acting*. Chicago: Dramatic Publishing Co., 1961. Taped interviews with John Gielgud, Sidney Poitier, Shelley Winters, Helen Hayes, Anne Bancroft, Bert Lahr.

Selected Scenes from Great Plays

These books contain scenes suitable for auditions or workshop projects.

Fedyszyn, Stan. *Scenes: For Actors*. Belmont, Calif.: Wadsworth Publishing Co., 1971, 244 pp.

Steffenson, James L., Jr. (ed.). *Great Scenes from the World Theatre*. New York: Avon Books, 1965. 576 pp.

Area Staging

This well-illustrated book is a brief but helpful guide to area staging of scenes and/or plays:

Boyle, Walden P. *Central and Flexible Staging: A New Theater in the Making*. Los Angeles: University of California Press, 1956. 117 pp.